SHANE MARQUIN VAN ROOYEN

The Last Supper's Call

Ends Human Trafficking and Children's Dissapearance

reedsy

Contents

Acknowledgement

Acknowledgment Letter

Dear Friends, Family, and Supporters,

I would like to take a moment to express my heartfelt gratitude to all those who have inspired and supported me throughout the journey of creating this book.

Your unwavering encouragement has been a driving force that propelled me forward, even when the task felt overwhelming.

I extend my sincere thanks to every character, individual, and friend who contributed their thoughts and insights to this project.

Your input has enriched my work in ways I cannot fully express.

A special acknowledgment goes to the Patriotic Alliances, whose embodiment of true humanity ignited my passion and purpose, during the time of Joslin Smith's disappearance. I am particularly grateful to the leader now Honorable Minister Gayton MacKenzie, a true and honest leader of the team for his guidance and input which inspired me to write this book.

I would also like to express my appreciation to Reedsy.com for their invaluable editing assistance, which allowed me to refine my work and present it in its best form. Additionally, I want to acknowledge The Open Door Evangelism & Outreach Ministry and every church and pastor whose teachings and support inspired me during the writing process.

Ultimately, this work was made possible through the knowledge, love, and unwavering support of The Holy Spirit.

Without Him, none of this would have been achievable, and for that, I am eternally grateful.

Thank you once again to everyone who played a part in this journey. Your influence and support mean the world to me. With heartfelt appreciation,

Shane Marquin van Rooyen

One

Chapter 1

* * *

On February 19, 2024, the shocking disappearance of a 6-year-old girl with green eyes in Saldanha, on South Africa's West Coast, sent shockwaves across the region, the continent, and the world. The entire community - every child, woman, and man - was gripped by the tragedy as the search began.

As I lay in my bed, mindlessly scrolling through my Facebook feed as I often did, a sudden image caught my eye

- a photo of a child, she had never seen before.

Immediately, a chill ran down my spine as I noticed the "Missing Child Alert" message attached to the post.

My heart began to race, pounding in my chest as a sense of

unease and urgency overcame on me.

It was as if some unseen force was jolting me awake, compelling me to pay closer attention to this distressing situation.

The child's piercing green eyes seemed to gaze directly into her soul, conveying a silent plea for help. Though the photo depicted a serene, sunlit scene, the girl's expression carried a profound sadness and desperation that belied the tranquil backdrop. This juxtaposition of the bright, idyllic setting and the child's haunting, pleading eyes created a striking contrast, hinting at the darker, more sinister circumstances that had likely led to her disappearance.

I found myself transported, my mind racing to imagine the young girl's plight - the fear, the uncertainty, the utter vulnerability of being torn from the safety and comfort of her home.

I could almost feel the child's anguish, the helplessness of being lost and alone, cut off from the warmth and security of her family. In that moment, my own world seemed to fade away, replaced by a deep, visceral empathy for this stranger's plight,

a profound need to uncover the truth and see the child safely returned to her loved ones. Me like any other person at the time not knowing the story behind the story. The weight of the unknown, the unanswered questions, hung heavy in the air, urging me to take action, through prayer and deeper connection with my creator to become part of the search, to lend my voice and my effort in prayer to bring this missing child home.

It's a familiar routine for me mindlessly scrolling through the endless stream of social media updates, occasionally pausing to read a story or leave a brief message of sympathy or concern.

But this time, as I were casually perusing my Facebook feed, a post caught my eye that immediately gave me to pause.

The simple, desperate plea "Help" stood out starkly against the background, instantly grabbing my attention and pulling me into the unfolding narrative. The details of the post that followed were chilling - a young child had vanished without a trace, disappearing in the blink of an eye in what was surely every parent's worst nightmare, I thought by myself . As I read on, I could feel the urgency and panic radiating through the words.

This was no ordinary post; it had clearly struck a chord, rapidly spreading across the platform and spurring an outpouring of concern. Thousands upon thousands of people, all united in shock and a desire to help, began mobilizing search efforts, sharing the child's photo, and doing everything in their power to assist in locating the missing girl. The story had gone viral, capturing the hearts and minds of a community desperate to bring this child safely home. No longer could you simply scroll past and move on - this was a crisis that demanded action, that compelled me to join the groundswell of support, to contribute what you could, to pray for the child's safe return. This was no longer just another story; it had become a clarion call to come together in the face of unimaginable tragedy.

This young child's story is a heartbreaking one, filled with the harsh realities that far too many innocent youths face in this world. Though she was just a small, naive child simply longing to live a normal, carefree life like any other kid, her fate took a devastating turn that she could never have anticipated. As a vulnerable, impressionable child who needed loving guidance, support, and protection, she instead found herself targeted and exploited by the dark forces of society - identity thieves, criminals, and others who seek to prey upon the most innocent and defenseless.

It's a tragic truth that children are often seen as attractive targets by those who would do them harm, their youth and innocence making them particularly vulnerable. This child's story serves as a sobering reminder that a parent's primary duty is to safeguard their child's well being - yet far too often, external circumstances or personal failings prevent them from fully doing so. In this case, the mother's own struggles, potentially including substance abuse issues, left her unable to provide the stable, nurturing environment this child so desperately needed.

As parents, we must always remember that children are constantly absorbing the behaviors and values modeled for them, whether positive or negative. Every choice we make, every action we take, sends a powerful message that shapes a young mind. It is our responsibility to lead by example, to demonstrate compassion, integrity, and resilience in the face of life's challenges. For this child, the lack of a strong, guiding parental influence left her adrift and exposed to untold dangers. Her story underscores the vital importance of parents being present, engaged, and proactive in safeguarding their children's wellbeing - for their today, and their tomorrow.

It's absolutely critical to ensure that you are not engaging in any kind of drug use, as substance abuse can have devastating and far-reaching consequences. If you have unfortunately fallen into the grips of addiction, it's imperative that you take immediate action to quit as soon as possible. Certain key factors can significantly increase the likelihood and speed at which someone develops a full-blown addiction. Chief among these is having a family history of addiction - research has shown that there is often a strong genetic component to substance abuse disorders, with individuals from families with a history of addiction being far more prone to developing addictions themselves. Mental health issues like depression, anxiety, or trauma can also greatly heighten the risk, as many turn to drugs and alcohol as a misguided attempt to self-medicate and numb their emotional pain. Peer pressure from friends and social circles that engage in drug use is another major contributing factor, as the normalization and encouragement of substance abuse makes it much harder for vulnerable individuals to resist. Additionally, a lack of strong family involvement and guidance during childhood and adolescence is associated with a higher chance of future addiction. Perhaps most alarmingly, even just experimenting with highly addictive drugs like heroin, cocaine, or methamphetamine can rapidly lead to a debilitating dependence that can destroy lives. Recognizing these risk factors and taking proactive steps to avoid or address them is absolutely vital to prevent the scourge of drug addiction from taking hold.

The disappearance of the young child was a tragic and perplexing mystery that captivated the attention of people across the globe. As the news of the missing six-year-old girl spread rapidly through the media, all eyes turned to the child's mother, who had filed the missing persons report with the local police just days earlier. The unsettling headline news painted a disturbing picture, alleging that this mother - the one who should have been the child's staunchest protector - had in fact been charged with the heinous crimes of trafficking and kidnapping. This shocking turn of events left the public reeling, desperate to understand how such a beautiful, innocent child could vanish without a trace, and how the very person who gave her life could somehow be complicit in her disappearance. The unanswered questions swirled - where was this child's mother when she went missing? What role, if any, did she play in the vanishing of her own flesh and blood? The details remained murky, but the implications were deeply troubling, casting a dark cloud of suspicion and mistrust over a tragedy that had already shattered so many hearts. As the investigation unfolded, the world waited with bated breath, hoping against hope that the child would be found safe, even as the growing evidence seemed to point an accusing finger squarely at the one person who should have protected her the most.

Reading a story like this, where a vulnerable individual has been subjected to such abhorrent abuse, is truly heartbreaking. It's deeply unsettling to confront the harsh reality that these horrific acts of exploitation can and do occur, often hidden from public view until a particular case is brought to light. While one hopes this is an isolated incident, the unfortunate truth is that such predatory behavior is far more widespread than we'd like to admit. The perpetrators can be anyone - a trusted family member, a close family friend, even someone within the victim's own household. And the manipulation and trauma inflicted upon these innocent victims is nothing short of pure evil. What's worse is that in many cases, previous instances of such abuse may have gone undetected, the victims silenced through fear, shame or a misplaced sense of loyalty. But in exposing this particular case, there is perhaps an opportunity to shine a light on this pervasive problem, to raise awareness and work towards preventative measures that can put a stop to the cycle of abuse before it continues. It's a sobering reminder of the darkness that can lurk beneath the surface of even the most seemingly stable and caring environments. Confronting this ugly truth head-on, as difficult as it may be, is the only way we can begin to make meaningful change and protect the vulnerable from such unspeakable harm.

I wrote this extraordinary book to share with you The Last Supper's Call around the this story and what I think God allowed this to happened.

The Last Supper is a pivotal event in the Christian faith, representing the final meal that Jesus shared with his disciples before his crucifixion. This sacred gathering holds profound theological significance, as it was during this intimate gathering that Jesus instituted the Eucharist, or Holy Communion, a sacrament that remains central to Christian worship and belief. During the Last Supper, Jesus broke bread and shared wine with his followers, declaring that the bread represented his body and the wine his blood - a symbolic foreshadowing of the sacrifice he would soon make on the cross. By partaking in this ritual, Jesus' disciples were called to remember his teachings, his unconditional love, and the new covenant he would establish through his death and resurrection. The Last Supper also serves as a poignant illustration of Jesus' profound humility, as he humbly washed the feet of his disciples, demonstrating the servant leadership he embodied. This final meal together was a profound moment of fellowship, as Jesus prepared his closest companions for the tumultuous events that were to unfold, urging them to remain steadfast in their faith. Even today, the Last Supper continues to be a source of deep spiritual reflection, reminding believers of the immense love and sacrifice at the heart of the Christian faith.

The Last Supper is a pivotal event in the Christian faith, representing the final meal that Jesus shared with his disciples before his crucifixion. This sacred gathering holds profound theological significance, as it was during this intimate gathering that Jesus instituted the Eucharist, or Holy Communion, a sacrament that remains central to Christian worship and belief. During the Last Supper, Jesus broke bread and shared wine with his followers, declaring that the bread represented his body and the wine his blood - a symbolic foreshadowing of the sacrifice he would soon make on the cross. By partaking in this ritual, Jesus' disciples were called to remember his teachings, his unconditional love, and the new covenant he would establish through his death and resurrection. The Last Supper also serves as a poignant illustration of Jesus' profound humility, as he humbly washed the feet of his disciples, demonstrating the servant leadership he embodied. This final meal together was a profound moment of fellowship, as Jesus prepared his closest companions for the tumultuous events that were to unfold, urging them to remain steadfast in their faith. Even today, the Last Supper continues to be a source of deep spiritual reflection, reminding believers of the immense love and sacrifice at the heart of the Christian faith.

While the comparison to the Last Supper may not be the most direct or obvious one, there is certainly a deeper spiritual and emotional resonance to be found in the story of the missing child. When we hear of a young, innocent life in peril, it naturally evokes a profound sense of concern and compassion within us - a yearning to reach out and provide comfort, sustenance, and protection, much as Christ did for his disciples during that final meal before his crucifixion.

As you described, sitting comfortably in your own home, enjoying a meal with your family, the contrast of this child's uncertain fate and potential lack of basic nourishment is deeply unsettling. It's a stark reminder of the fragility of life and the harsh realities that some must face, through no fault of their own. In that moment, the lines between your own privileged circumstances and the child's dire straits become starkly clear, stirring up feelings of empathy, guilt, and an urgent need to intercede on their behalf.

Just as the Last Supper represented a pivotal turning point, a solemn precursor to Christ's ultimate sacrifice, the search for this missing child has galvanized an entire community - people of all faiths and backgrounds uniting in a common quest to locate and protect one of their own. It is a powerful testament to the unifying force of compassion, and the profound capacity of the human spirit to rise above individual differences in service of a greater good.

In this way, the divine grace embodied by the Last Supper, with its promises of forgiveness, salvation, and eternal life, finds a contemporary parallel in the fervent prayers and collective efforts surrounding this child's safe return. It is a reminder that, regardless of our specific beliefs, we are all bound by a shared humanity and an innate desire to care for one another, especially the most vulnerable among us. The hand of God, as you so eloquently observed, is indeed moving in mysterious and profound ways, calling us to set aside our differences and come together in unity, empowered by faith and fueled by love.

In this remarkable situation, I witnessed a truly remarkable display of unity and faith come together, transcending the boundaries of individual beliefs and backgrounds. People from all walks of life, with diverse religious and cultural affiliations, put aside their differences to join in a collective effort - not just to pray, but to actively search and work towards a common goal. It was as if a higher power had called this community to action, uniting them in a shared purpose that eclipsed any divisions. The hand of God seemed to move through this crisis, galvanizing the masses and inspiring them to put aside their own agendas in order to focus solely on finding the missing child. There was a palpable sense that something profound was unfolding, a divine orchestration that had brought these disparate elements together in a spirit of compassion and determination.

Just as the Lord's Supper serves as a poignant reminder of Christ's life and sacrifice, binding believers through the new covenant, this community's collective response mirrored that sacred unity. Their actions became a living testament to the transformative power of love and faith, a taste of the ultimate heavenly feast to come. In the midst of darkness and uncertainty, they found solace and strength in supporting one another, heeding the commandment to love as Jesus had loved. And in the end, this story of Joslin Smith became a profound lesson - a testament to the transformative power of setting aside our differences to embrace our shared humanity, and to love one another as we have been loved.

Those who commit the unthinkable act of harming a child, whether through abduction, abuse, or any other heinous means, have clearly lost touch with the divine love and compassion that should reside in the hearts of all humanity. To extinguish the life or wellbeing of an innocent child is to reject the very essence of what it means to be human - to nurture, protect, and cherish the most vulnerable among us. It is a betrayal of the sacred trust placed in us as caregivers and community members. Without that foundation of love and empathy, one's soul becomes an empty vessel, devoid of the qualities that give life meaning and purpose. No matter the justification or rationale used to explain such abhorrent behavior, the inescapable truth remains that to choose cruelty over kindness, to sever the unbreakable bond between adult and child, is to willfully disconnect oneself from the grace of the divine and the inherent dignity of human life. It is a descent into the darkest realms of the human condition, where the light of compassion has been extinguished, leaving only a void that can never be filled. For those who have committed such unforgivable acts, the love of God and their fellow man has been cast aside, leaving them adrift in a sea of their own making, forever severed from the very essence of what it means to be truly alive.

The Bible says, If I speak in the tongues of men and of angels, but have not love, I am only a resounding gong or a clanging cymbal. 1Corinthians 13

In this world, there are those who seem to derive a twisted sense of pleasure from inflicting pain and humiliation upon others, a disturbing phenomenon that can be described as sadism. These individuals, often referred to as sadists or psychopaths, exhibit a complete lack of empathy or remorse, callously disregarding the suffering they cause. Their actions stand in stark contrast to the principles laid out in the sacred texts, such as the Bible, which call upon followers to adhere strictly to the law and to conduct themselves with virtue and compassion. The book of Joshua, for instance, instructs the faithful to meditate on the word of God day and night, ensuring that they act in accordance with all that is written, for only then will they find true prosperity and success. Yet, the sadist brazenly flouts these divine commandments, prioritizing their own warped gratification over the wellbeing of their fellow human beings. This type of behavior is wholly unacceptable in the eyes of the Almighty, for it

The Law was given by God not as a means to make men righteous, but rather to expose the sinful nature of humanity. Through the commandments and statutes laid out in the Law, God was graciously shining a light on the reality that no person is capable of perfectly obeying and fulfilling the divine standards set before them. The Law, in all its lofty and holy requirements, served to make it abundantly clear that mankind is inherently flawed, fallen, and incapable of achieving the level of righteousness demanded by a perfect and just God. Rather than providing a path to earned salvation, the Law was intended to humble people and reveal their desperate need for an imputed righteousness - a righteousness that could not be achieved through one's own efforts and obedience, but could only be granted as a free gift of grace through faith in Jesus Christ. By declaring the full weight and gravity of the Law, God was ultimately being gracious, for He was showing humanity the hopelessness of self-righteousness and the absolute necessity of relying on the perfect, substitutionary work of the Messiah. The commandments, from "Thou shalt have no other gods before me" to the entirety of the Mosaic code, were never meant to make people righteous, but to drive them to the only One who could - the Lord Jesus, whose righteousness is freely offered to all who believe.

The Ten Commandments set forth a moral and ethical framework that has guided societies for centuries, providing a clear blueprint for righteous living. Yet, as the passage notes, it is all too common for individuals to fall short of upholding these sacred tenets. "Thou shalt not make unto thee any graven image" instructs against the worship of false idols, commanding us to direct our reverence solely towards the divine. Similarly, "Thou shalt not take the name of the Lord thy God in vain" cautions against using the Almighty's name flippantly or irreverently. The commandment to "Remember the sabbath day, to keep it holy" establishes a sacred day of rest and reflection, a time to reconnect with our spiritual selves. "Honour thy father and thy mother" is a fundamental tenet of family and community, reinforcing the importance of respecting our elders and origins. "Thou shalt not kill" is an unequivocal prohibition on the taking of human life, safeguarding the sanctity of existence. "Thou shalt not commit adultery" upholds the sanctity of marriage and faithful, monogamous relationships. Lastly, "Thou shalt not steal" protects the property and possessions of others, ensuring a just and orderly society. While it is true that we often fall short of perfectly upholding these commandments, that does not negate their profound significance or our obligation to strive towards that higher moral standard. Rather than using our own failings as an excuse to harm others, we must recommit ourselves to living with integrity, compassion, and reverence for the divine principles that undergird a meaningful, virtuous life.

The tragic story of Joshlin Smith has left many in the small coastal town of Saldanha on the West Coast of the country deeply unsettled. Whispers abound that the young woman may have fallen victim to a dark and sinister fate, potentially being sold to local Sangomas for use in some sort of ritual purpose. However, the full truth of what happened to Joshlin remains shrouded in mystery, as an ongoing court case involving four suspects continues to unfold behind closed doors.

Sangomas, also known as inyangas, occupy a revered and powerful position within many Bantu communities across Southern Africa. These shamans, healers, and spiritual leaders have served as the backbone of traditional practices and beliefs for generations, wielding profound knowledge of herbal remedies, divination, and connection to the supernatural realm. Yet, as rapid Westernization sweeps the region, the old ways of the Sangomas are rapidly eroding, replaced by the allure of the modern commodity market.

In the case of Joshlin's disappearance, the involvement of these Sangomas is only rumored, not confirmed. But the very mention of their name evokes a deep unease, for the Sangomas are believed to possess the ability to tap into dark, primordial forces that exist beyond the mortal plane. As one local resident solemnly reflects, "the light of God is a reality, but the darkness of the devil is also a reality. People do strange and unspeakable things in life, for they are controlled by powers not of this world."

Indeed, the forces of darkness are ever-present, lurking in the shadows and waiting to ensnare the unwary. By delving into their own inner darkness, some believe that the Sangomas can interface with these malevolent energies, harnessing a well of potential that transcends the boundaries of the physical realm. And it is this terrifying prospect that has the community on edge, as they anxiously await the outcome of the ongoing trial, praying that the truth of Joshlin's fate will finally be revealed.

In my previous book "The Missing Piece, the Whole in My Heart," I candidly recounted my previous involvement with Satanism and the profound impact it had on my life. This deeply personal account shed light on the dangers and consequences of delving into the occult. As I so poignantly described, Satanism can exert a seductive, corrupting influence, leading one down a dark path of spiritual and emotional turmoil. The case of Joslin's mysterious disappearance, which I discussed, serves as a sobering example of how the forces of darkness can wreak havoc in people's lives. Yet, through this tragedy, important truths have been illuminated - truths that we must heed and learn from.

Thankfully, my book also reminds us of the unwavering promise found in God's word - that He will never abandon us, no matter how bleak the circumstances may seem. For there is nothing that can ever be hidden from the all-knowing, all-powerful gaze of the divine. In His perfect timing, He will bring every secret, every misdeed, out into the light, so that we may find the healing and redemption that only He can provide. My story stands as a powerful testament to the transformative power of turning away from the darkness and embracing the light of God's love and grace.

Two

Chapter 2

During this tumultuous period, the close-knit community of Saldahna on the rugged west coast of South Africa was gripped by a desperate search, as they fervently scoured the land and scanned the horizon day and night, driven by the fervent hope of finding their lost little green-eyed angel. This young child, whose innocent gaze had so tenderly captured the hearts of many within the community, had vanished without a trace, leaving a profound void that echoed through the very fabric of their close-knit seaside town. Neighbors banded together, combing the beaches and dunes, peering into every nook and cranny, their voices carrying a palpable mix of determination and anguish as they called out the child's name, praying for any sign of their beloved missing treasure. The typically tranquil streets of Saldahna were now alive with a palpable sense of unease, as residents young and old alike joined the tireless search, their eyes scanning the horizon with a mixture of hope and dread, desperate to be the one to finally locate the green-eyed angel who had so deeply embedded themselves in the communal consciousness. This was a time of profound uncertainty and anguish, as the community rallied together, their collective heartbeat a cacophony of prayers and pleas, all united in the fervent desire to bring their lost little one safely home.

The story of the Saldahna community's plight and the out-pouring of support from far and wide was truly a magnificent testament to the power of human compassion and the guiding hand of the divine. People from all corners of the region flocked to lend their aid, driven by a deep-seated desire to uplift and comfort their fellow citizens in a time of unimaginable anguish. It was as if an invisible thread connected the hearts of this community to the greater whole, transcending geographical boundaries and uniting them in a shared purpose.

For those who bore witness, it was a profound revelation of the ways in which God can work through the collective efforts of His flock. Though the tragedy that befell this community was shrouded in mystery and heartbreak, the faithful found solace in the belief that the Almighty had a greater plan at work - one that would ultimately lead them to a place of healing and renewed purpose. In their darkest hour, the people of Saldahna were reminded that they were never truly alone, for the divine presence was woven into the very fabric of their struggle.

Indeed, it is in times of great adversity that the true nature of God's love is often most clearly revealed. When we find ourselves tempted to push the Almighty aside, He has a remark-able way of inserting Himself into our lives, demanding our attention and guiding us back to the path of righteousness. In the case of the Saldahna community, it was the disappearance of a young, innocent life that served as the catalyst, drawing the nation's gaze and stirring the collective soul to action.

Whether through a restless spirit, a vague dissatisfaction, or the unthinkable loss of a child, God has a remarkable ability to captivate our attention and redirect it towards the higher purpose that He has ordained. And as the people of Saldahna discovered, when we open our hearts to His will, we are granted the privilege of witnessing the divine at work, unfolding in ways that humble and inspire us. It is a testament to the boundless love and wisdom of our Creator, who never ceases to find new ways to draw us closer to Him.

In the midst of our busy, hectic lives, it's easy to become distracted and lose sight of what truly matters. We can get so caught up in the day-to-day grind, dwelling on past hurts and disappointments or anxiously worrying about the future, that we fail to be present and attentive to God's work in our lives in the here and now. Yet it is often in those unexpected moments - when a passage of Scripture resonates with us in a new way, or a chance remark from a friend gives us pause - that God gently intervenes to redirect our focus. These divine "whistles" can take many forms, from the trials of illness, financial troubles, or personal tragedies, to the disappointments and failures that leave us feeling lost and adrift. In our pain and confusion, it becomes all too tempting to shut ourselves off, to nurse our wounds and wallow in negativity rather than opening ourselves up to God's presence and guidance. But it is precisely in these moments of difficulty that the Lord is seeking to meet with us, to speak truth and offer comfort, if only we will be still and attentive. You see, God does not dwell in some distant future, but moves and works in the present moment - it is here, in the here and now, that He desires to shape our steps and determine our path forward. If we become so preoccupied with the past or so anxious about what is to come that we fail to recognize and respond to His voice in the present, we risk missing out on the help, the wisdom, and the profound peace that He longs to impart. In the end, it is our willingness to pause, to listen, and to open ourselves up to God in the midst of our circumstances that allows us to experience His transformative power at work, guiding us through the trials of life and ushering us into a deeper, more intimate relationship with Him.

At the time of Joslin's disappearance, our country was embroiled in a state of turmoil and upheaval. The newspapers, media, television programs, radio broadcasts, and social media were rife with accounts of the many crises unfolding across the nation. Corruption had seemingly taken hold, with stories emerging of children dying on the streets, murders occurring on isolated farms, and the scourge of human trafficking victimizing the most vulnerable. Missing children cases were sadly common, while the lack of jobs and the proliferation of gangs and drugs painted a bleak picture. Tragically, people were even shooting one another with alarming frequency, in what seemed to be a legal free-for-all. Robberies of homes and businesses were occurring on a daily basis, leaving citizens feeling unsafe and helpless in the face of this societal disaster. It was a dark and chaotic time, where the very fabric of the country appeared to be unraveling before the eyes of its citizens. Amidst this backdrop of crisis and lawlessness, Joslin's disappearance only added to the sense of unease and uncertainty gripping the nation.

In a seemingly unexpected turn of events, God Himself made a profound call that shook the nation to its core. This call, one that nobody could have foreseen, brought the entire country to a standstill as everyone became more alert and attentive to one another. What was so striking about this divine intervention was that the disappearance of a young girl named Joslin seemed to be the catalyst. Though Joslin was tragically not the only child to go missing, her case somehow went viral, capturing the attention of the masses in a way that previous cases had not. This divine orchestration was surely no coincidence - it was God's way of conveying a powerful message, a message that "enough is enough."

Prior to this pivotal moment, many other missing children had simply become faceless files, their cases eventually abandoned by authorities who had reached a point of hopelessness. Some were fortunately found, alive or deceased, while others remained elusive, lost to the shadows or potentially subjected to unspeakable fates. It was as if these individual tragedies had been quietly swept aside, their urgency fading from public consciousness. But with Joslin's case thrusting the issue into the national spotlight, God seized the opportunity to deliver a thunderous proclamation - a call for action that would echo around the world, demanding that this epidemic of missing and exploited children be brought to an end. The time had come for divine intervention, for God to stretch forth His mighty hand and say, in no uncertain terms, that this grave injustice could no longer be tolerated. Through the singular tragedy of Joslin, the Almighty had chosen this nation to be the vessel for

His resounding message: "Enough is enough."

The intricate workings of the divine are often shrouded in mystery, beyond the full comprehension of the human mind. As the scripture from Ecclesiastes 11:5 so poignantly states, "As you do not know the way the spirit comes to the bones in the womb of a woman with child, so you do not know the work of God who makes everything." This profound verse speaks to the inherent unknowability of God's grand design and the humbling limitations of our own understanding. Just as the miraculous process of life unfolding within the mother's womb remains a profound enigma, the greater tapestry of how the Almighty orchestrates all of creation is ultimately inscrutable to us. We can glimpse fragments, observe patterns, and draw insights, but the totality of God's workings exists on a plane that transcends our finite perspective. This scripture urges us to approach the divine with a posture of reverence and humility, acknowledging that the ways of the Lord are higher than our ways, and His thoughts are beyond our ability to fully grasp. In the face of such awesome mystery, we are called to trust implicitly in the sovereignty of the Maker, who weaves the threads of the universe with a wisdom that exceeds our comprehension. Though we may never fully fathom the intricate mechanisms by which God brings about His will, we can take solace in the assurance that His work is perfect, and His purposes will ultimately be fulfilled, even when shrouded in the shadows of our limited understanding.

This tragic situation speaks to the profound and mysterious ways in which God orchestrates the course of our lives, even when they take unexpected and heartbreaking turns. Though the disappearance of young Joslin Smith was a devastating loss that shocked her community and the world, it was all part of a greater plan ordained by the Almighty long before any of us were born. In the blink of an eye, this child who was previously unknown became a household name, not for the tragic circumstances of her vanishing, but for the divine purpose she was destined to fulfill.

Though we may never fully understand why such tragedies occur, or why God allows innocent lives to be taken, we must trust that there is a higher reasoning at work. The grief, anger, and sense of injustice we feel in the face of such senseless loss is understandable and human - it speaks to our innate longing for a world filled with peace, harmony, and compassion for one another. Yet amidst the darkness, we are reminded that God is ever-present, guiding events according to His inscrutable plan. Even when it seems that evil and indifference have triumphed, we can take solace in the knowledge that the Almighty is working to set all things right in the end.

Though the disappearance of Joslin Smith was undoubtedly a devastating tragedy, it was part of a greater tapestry woven by the divine hand. In time, the true meaning and purpose of her life and untimely demise will be revealed, reminding us that there is always more at work in this world than meets the eye. While we may mourn the loss of one so young and innocent, we can find comfort in the certainty that God is sovereign, and that even the most heartbreaking events are part of His perfect plan.

The Book of Job in the Bible tells a powerful story of a man who was tested and tried in the most extreme ways, yet emerged with an even stronger faith in God. When the devil sought to rip Job's life apart, stripping him of his wealth, family, and health, God allowed it to happen, not to punish Job, but to ultimately rebuild his future in an even more profound way. As the passage describes, we cannot always comprehend the full reasoning behind God's actions - the ways in which he allows his faithful followers to endure such immense suffering and hardship. Yet, the lesson of Job's story is one of unwavering trust, even in the face of unimaginable pain and loss. Though the journey may be thorny and the path arduous, the faithful must press on in steadfast belief that there is a greater purpose at work, that God has a plan to restore and rebuild what has been torn asunder. The process may be agonizing, the wait for redemption and renewal agonizingly slow, but the faithful must cling to the promise that there is meaning and reason behind even the darkest of trials. Just as Job's future was ultimately remade stronger than before, so too can the faithful be rebuilt and restored, if they maintain their trust in the divine wisdom that lies beyond their own limited understanding. It is a message of hope amidst suffering, of renewal after devastation - a testament to the power of faith to carry us through even the most shattering of circumstances.

In the matter of Joslin Smith, it was truly a profound and moving experience to witness the outpouring of concern and divine intervention from the community. What began as a distressing situation quickly transformed into a daily vigil, as people from all walks of life came together through social media to support the search efforts. The online platforms became a hub of activity, with constant updates, pleas for information, and an overwhelming sense of unity in the face of uncertainty. It was as if a divine presence had enveloped the entire situation, guiding the search and uniting the hearts and minds of everyone involved. Each post, each share, each comment was imbued with a tangible feeling of hope and faith, as if a higher power was orchestrating events beyond our mortal understanding. The outreach and solidarity displayed online reflected a community that had transcended the boundaries of geography and background, all focused on the singular mission of finding Joslin and bringing her home safely. In the darkest of moments, the collective energy of prayers, positive affirmations, and unwavering determination became a beacon of light, illuminating the path forward and reminding everyone that even in the face of adversity, the power of community and the presence of the divine can provide solace and inspiration. It was a truly humbling and awe-inspiring experience to witness the seamless merging of human compassion and divine intervention in the search for Joslin Smith. In times of great injustice and oppression, there have always been courageous individuals who have risen up to defend the voiceless and advocate for the vulnerable. Such was the case with the remarkable people that God raised up to stand up for a child who could not speak for herself. These righteous champions recognized the inherent dignity and worth of this young, defenseless soul, and were compelled by a higher moral calling to be her voice and safeguard her from harm. Through their tireless efforts and unwavering commitment, they navigated complex legal and social systems, challenged entrenched power structures, and relentlessly pursued justice on her behalf. Their strength in the face of adversity, their compassion in the midst of cruelty, and their refusal to be silenced in the wake of indifference served as a shining example of the transformative power of faith, courage, and the indomitable human spirit. In championing the cause of one child, they spoke for all those who have been marginalized, exploited, and denied their most fundamental rights - reminding us that the true measure of a society lies in how it treats its most vulnerable members. Through their heroic actions, these exceptional individuals etched their names in the annals of history, having answered the divine call to be vessels of hope, beacons of justice, and advocates for the voiceless in a time of great darkness and despair.

In a surprising turn of events, the divine hand of God intervened in the political sphere, granting a unique opportunity to Gayton MacKenzie, a prominent politician and party leader. Alongside his trusted assistant, Ashley Sauls, MacKenzie found himself entrusted with a divine mandate – to ensure that a certain search, the details of which remain shrouded in mystery, would never be allowed to reach its conclusion. The weight of this responsibility, bestowed upon them by a higher power, must have been both humbling and daunting, as the two individuals were now tasked with navigating the complex world of politics and public opinion, all while heeding the call of a force greater than themselves. One can only imagine the conversations and strategies that unfolded between MacKenzie and Sauls, as they grappled with the implications of this divine intervention and sought to fulfill their sacred duty, come what may. The very fact that God Himself had chosen to involve Himself in the affairs of the mortal realm underscores the gravity of the situation, and the profound impact it must have had on the lives and decisions of those entrusted with this weighty charge. As the search continued, one can envision the unwavering determination and resourcefulness that MacKenzie and Sauls would have needed to employ, leveraging their political acumen and the power of their faith to ensure that the mandated course of action was upheld, no matter the obstacles that arose along the way. The issue they are addressing has long been a contentious and polarizing one, with many staunchly opposing any progress or change. However, this group of advocates is steadfast in their conviction that it will not be allowed to simply become another "closed file" that is forgotten and relegated to the sidelines as has happened in the past. They recognize the sensitive and politically-charged nature of the topic, but firmly believe that this is fundamentally a matter of basic human rights and dignity, not a political game to be played. While their opponents have tried to paint them as having a hidden agenda or ulterior motive, the group maintains that their sole driving force is a genuine, heartfelt compassion for their fellow human beings who are suffering. They refuse to be silenced or deterred by accusations of politicizing the issue, understanding that sometimes the most meaningful and impactful change can only come when people are willing to courageously advocate for what is right, even in the face of criticism and resistance. This group is steadfast in their commitment to seeing this cause through, no matter the obstacles, driven by an unwavering belief that every person deserves to be treated with the utmost respect and have their fundamental needs met. They will not back down, for they know that the stakes are simply too high to allow this issue to be swept under the rug once again.

Amidst the swirling chaos and uncertainty surrounding the disappearance of the child, the dedicated investigators press on, undaunted by the challenges that lie before them. Though the reasons that initially prompted this arduous search may have become obscured by the mounting pressures and emotional turmoil, their commitment to finding the missing child remains steadfast. From the very moment the child vanished, these tireless professionals have poured their heart and soul into the investigation, leaving no stone unturned in their relentless pursuit of answers. Each lead, no matter how tenuous, is meticulously followed up, each witness interviewed with the utmost care and diligence. The team works tirelessly around the clock, scouring the local community and beyond for any shred of information that could help guide them to the child's safe return. Sifting through mountains of evidence, analyzing every scrap of data, they remain undeterred, driven by an unwavering determination to bring this child home. Though the path ahead is shrouded in uncertainty, these investigators press on, fueled by an unwavering sense of duty and the belief that their efforts will ultimately lead them to the answers they seek, no matter how long it takes. Ashley Sauls was one of the tireless and dedicated members of the community who immediately sprang into action to help search for the missing person, without a moment's rest. From the very first day the person disappeared, Ashley was out there alongside countless others, scouring the area day and night in an all-consuming effort to locate them. The upcoming elections in May 2024 were fast approaching, but Ashley and the other volunteers put aside any campaigning or political obligations they may have had, recognizing that finding the missing individual was the top priority. They worked around the clock, braving the elements and pushing through exhaustion, driven by an unwavering determination to bring this person home safely. The search parties combed every inch of the nearby woods and neighborhoods, not leaving a single stone unturned in their desperate hunt. Ashley's commitment was absolute - they refused to give up hope, even as the hours stretched into days with no sign of the missing person. This was a true community effort, with Ashley at the forefront, selflessly dedicating themselves to the cause without a moment's hesitation. It was a profound display of human compassion and the power of a community coming together in a time of crisis.

As I began to listen intently to the divine, I felt a profound stirring within my spirit.

The weight of the challenges facing my nation had driven me to seek solace and guidance from the Almighty, pouring my heart out in fervent prayer.

With a deep longing to receive answers, I committed myself wholeheartedly to this pursuit, determined to forge an unwavering connection with the Almighty.

In the stillness of my moments of supplication, I felt a palpable shift - the veil parting, as it were, to unveil the whispers of the divine.

And there, in that sacred space, I heard it - the unmistakable voice of God, reassuring me with the simple, yet profound declaration: "I have a plan." In that instant, I perspective shifted, transcending the chaos and uncertainty that had previously consumed my thoughts. I realized that while the course of events may have seemed opaque and unfathomable to the human eye, the Almighty was orchestrating a divine strategy, one that would unfold in due time. Though the specifics of this plan remained shrouded, I found solace in the unwavering certainty that God was indeed at work, moving in ways that may have been imperceptible to the mortal mind, but were nevertheless guided by a wisdom and purpose far beyond my own understanding.

In that moment, I was filled with a profound trust, a deep-seated conviction that the Almighty was in control, and that His plan would ultimately bring about the restoration and redemption my nation so desperately needed.

In that moment, it was clear that God was orchestrating a profound sequence of events, though the full significance would not be immediately apparent to those bearing witness. The disappearance of a young 6-year-old child had shaken the community, and yet there was an unmistakable sense that this tragedy was not merely a random occurrence, but rather a catalyst for a greater divine purpose. As the search efforts intensified and political leaders became increasingly involved, it struck me that there was a deeper spiritual undercurrent at play. For too long, God had been excluded from the realm of politics in South Africa, relegated to the periphery as secular forces dominated the public discourse. But now, in the midst of this heartbreaking situation, the Almighty was making His presence known, compelling even the highest echelons of power to confront questions of faith and morality that had long been avoided. It was as if God was issuing a clarion call, a reminder that He cannot be confined to the private sphere but must be central to the decisions and actions that shape the very fabric of society. In the disappearance of this young child, a window had been opened, allowing the divine to penetrate the halls of influence and leadership, challenging them to acknowledge the profound spiritual realities that undergird our world. Though the path ahead may have seemed shrouded in mystery, there was a palpable sense that God was moving in powerful ways, reclaiming His rightful place in the political and social discourse of the nation.

Ashley Saul's, known affectionately by his community as "Oom Biza van die Kaap," had a long and complex history with God. Once a pastor himself, he had stepped away from that role for reasons known only to him and the divine. Yet, despite this change in his outward circumstances, his relationship with the Almighty remained steadfast and deeply personal. Oom Biza understood the intricacies of this bond in a way that few others could, having weathered the highs and lows, the moments of clarity and the periods of uncertainty, that inevitably come with walking such a spiritual path.

And now, at the behest of his political leader, the President of the Patriotic Alliance party, Oom Biza found himself on a new quest - a searching mission that consumed his days and nights as he rallied his community to join him. Together they scoured the land, driven by an unseen force that compelled them onward. But as the hours turned to days, and the days blurred into weeks, that divine presence they sought remained stubbornly silent, leaving Oom Biza and his devoted followers to wonder if they had somehow strayed from the path that God had laid out before them.

Yet, through it all, Oom Biza maintained his faith, his certainty that the Almighty had indeed called him to this task, even if the reasons remained shrouded in mystery. He knew, deep within his soul, that he had been chosen for this moment, this time, and that the answers he sought would reveal themselves in due course, if only he and his community remained steadfast in their search. For Oom Biza, the journey was not about the destination, but about the sacred process of discovery, of allowing God's will to unfold in its own time, even when the silence seemed deafening and the way forward uncertain.

The community was in a state of profound distress, their collective voices echoing through the streets as they desperately cried out for their missing child, Joslin. Day and night, the name "Joslin" reverberated through the air, a piercing plea that seemed to reach the very heavens above. It was as if the mere utterance of this name held a deep, almost spiritual significance - a reflection of a fervent plea for help in a time of great need.

The anguished cries did not simply fade into the background, but rather took on an almost tangible quality, becoming a palpable force that permeated the atmosphere. With each shout of "Where is our child? We want our Joslin!", the sense of urgency and desperation grew, painting a vivid picture of a community united in their quest to locate their missing loved one. The name "Joslin" became a beacon, a rallying cry that evoked a profound sense of personal connection, as if anyone who heard it was being called upon to join the search and offer their aid.

As time passed and Joslin remained elusive, the community's pleas took on an almost eternal quality, echoing through the ages and across the heavens. It was as if the very fabric of the universe had been imbued with the sorrow and desperation of those searching, the name "Joslin" becoming a universal call for divine intervention. And then, just when all seemed lost, a glimmer of hope emerged, as Ashley Sauls received a divine instruction to gather the church and address this pressing matter. The search for Joslin had become a sacred quest, one that would now be taken up by the faithful, guided by the hand of God himself.

The name "Joslin" carried a profound significance, evoking a profound sense of divine aid and intervention. Whenever this name passed through the lips of those who spoke it, it was as if a silent plea for heavenly assistance was being uttered. The very utterance of this name seemed to summon the power and grace of the Almighty, a symbolic gesture of humility and reliance on a higher authority. As time unfolded, a woman named Ashley Sauls found herself at a crossroads, guided by what she believed to be a direct instruction from God. She had been called to gather the Church, to unite the faithful in addressing a matter of great importance. But the question lingered - where was the Church to be found in this pivotal moment? Was it a physical congregation, a scattered community of believers, or something deeper and more transcendent? Ashley grappled with this query, knowing that the answer held the key to fulfilling the divine directive that had been entrusted to her. The name Joslin, with its inherent connotations of divine aid, seemed to hover over her, a constant reminder that she was not alone in her quest, and that the guidance of a higher power was available to her, if she but had the courage to seek it out and heed its call. This was a moment of spiritual reckoning, a test of faith and purpose, where the very essence of the Church and its role in the world would be revealed to Ashley, if she had the wisdom and discernment to perceive it.

The topic I've described points to a profound spiritual awakening and call to action from the divine.

Apparently, there has been a divine urging for the church to return to its true purpose and role in society.

God is seen as desiring the church to step up, to engage in fervent prayer, and to become deeply involved in the affairs of the nation once more. This suggests a time of great spiritual intensity and revival is upon us. The sense is that for too long, there has been division and discord - within the church, the government, and society at large. But God is now moving to bring about a restoration of unity, harmony, and divine purpose. Interestingly, this shift seems to be connected to the disappearance of a key figure, Joslin Smith, which has perhaps served as a catalyst for this spiritual awakening. The implication is that God is using this event to rally the church and the nation, calling them to a place of greater alignment with His will and vision. There is an air of excitement and anticipation, as this divine intervention is poised to transform the spiritual and sociopolitical landscape in profound ways. The stage is set for a remarkable season of spiritual renewal and national unity, as God reasserts His sovereignty and calling over His people.

The unity and oneness that Jesus prayed for in John 17:21 is a profound and powerful concept. When we are united in Christ, it creates a powerful witness to the world around us. This unity is not just a surface-level agreement, but a deep, spiritual connection where we are "one" with the Father, just as Jesus is one with the Father. It's a unity that transcends our differences and allows us to come together in a way that reflects the very nature of the Godhead.

This call to unity was highlighted during the Last Supper, as Jesus knew His betrayal and crucifixion were imminent. In Matthew 26, we see Jesus foretelling that one of His own disciples would betray Him. Yet, even in the face of this impending tragedy, Jesus' focus remained on the unity of His followers. He wanted them to be "one" so that the world would believe that the Father had sent Him. Jesus recognized that disunity and division would undermine the credibility of His message, but that true, Spirit-empowered unity would be a powerful apologetic for the truth of the gospel.

All we have to do is heed this call and work towards the solution that God has provided - to surrender ourselves fully to Christ and allow His Spirit to bind us together in supernatural unity. This is no easy task, as our natural tendency is towards selfishness and division. But when we make the choice to die to ourselves and live for the greater good of the body, we tap into the transformative power that Jesus prayed for. A watching world will take notice when they see believers who are truly "one" in Christ.

The Last Supper was a pivotal moment in the life and ministry of Jesus Christ, marking the final gathering of Jesus with his twelve disciples before his crucifixion. As described in the biblical accounts, the scene unfolds with a sense of solemn anticipation - the disciples coming to Jesus to make preparations for the Passover meal, Jesus providing specific instructions to them, and the group then assembling in the evening to partake in this sacred ritual together. But as they recline at the table, a dark cloud descends over the proceedings when Jesus solemnly declares that one of them will betray him. This shocking revelation elicits an outpouring of distress and self-doubt from the disciples, each one questioning whether they could be the one to commit such a grave act of treachery. Jesus then identifies the betrayer as the one who has dipped his hand into the bowl with him, a symbolic gesture that underscores the intimacy and trust that has been violated. Though Judas tries to deflect suspicion, Jesus affirms that he is indeed the one who will hand him over to his enemies. Against this ominous backdrop, Jesus then institutes the Eucharist, breaking bread and sharing wine as a representation of his body and blood that will soon be sacrificed. His words about not drinking of the vine until the coming of his Father's kingdom lend a sense of finality to the proceedings, as Jesus and his disciples depart to the Mount of Olives, where the events leading to the Crucifixion will soon unfold. The Last Supper, then, stands as a poignant and solemn moment, where the sacred and the profane, the divine and the human, collide in a charged and emotionally-charged setting, foreshadowing the momentous events to come.

Betrayal is a deeply painful and disorienting experience that occurs when a person we have put our trust in intentionally violates that trust, often in a way that causes us significant harm. Whether it's a close friend revealing our most intimate secrets, a romantic partner being unfaithful, or a family member deceiving us, the sense of betrayal can be devastating. It strikes at the very core of our ability to feel safe and secure in our relationships, leaving us feeling vulnerable, foolish, and bitterly disappointed. Betrayal often involves a breach of confidentiality, a lack of loyalty, or outright dishonesty - and it can manifest in both actions and omissions, when someone fails to act in a way that upholds our trust. As human beings, we are called to live in harmony, to support and care for one another, and to build bonds of mutual trust. Yet time and again, we fall short of this ideal, succumbing to our baser impulses and allowing selfishness, greed, or a misguided sense of self-interest to erode the trust at the heart of our relationships. The pain of betrayal is a profound reminder of our human fallibility, our capacity for cruelty, and the fragility of the connections that give our lives meaning. But it is also a call to recommit ourselves to the hard work of building authentic, trustworthy relationships - to be the kind of people worthy of others' faith in us.

In a remarkable display of unwavering faith and divine purpose, two extraordinary men embarked on a mission to seek out the elusive Joslin Smith. Oom Biza vannie Kaap and Gayton MacKenzie, called by God to go beyond borders and do whatever it took, tirelessly pursued this quest. Driven by a higher purpose, they were not deterred by obstacles or skepticism, for they knew their actions were guided by the Almighty. Alongside them, God had assembled a formidable team of spiritual leaders, including the esteemed Leo dos Santos, Pastor Koffie (also known as Fransico), and the renowned Prophet Jay Jay. These great men of God, united in their devotion, stood resolute in the face of adversity, determined to see the fulfillment of God's greater plan.

Despite the whispers of gossip and the judgmental murmurings of the church, the unwavering faith of this chosen group remained steadfast. They understood that their calling was not by accident, but by divine design – God had orchestrated every step of their journey, knowing the ultimate outcome would be a testament to His power and grace. As they pressed on, undeterred by the naysayers, their unwavering commitment and unshakable belief in God's plan inspired and galvanized the community around them. This was no mere coincidence, but a deliberate and purposeful movement, guided by the hand of the Almighty, to see His greater vision come to fruition in a remarkable display of faith, perseverance, and the unbreakable bond between devoted believers.

From the eyes of the flesh, Gayton MacKenzie's actions may have appeared to be an intervention or disruption of the natural order, but when viewed through the lens of faith, it becomes clear that he was simply following the divine calling placed upon his life. Though his choices and behaviors may have seemed unorthodox or even controversial to the casual observer, the underlying truth was that the plan was always in the hands of a Greater Power. Gayton's role was not to devise his own agenda, but to humbly submit to the will of God and allow the Almighty to work out the details according to a higher purpose. In the end, despite any initial skepticism or opposition, it became evident that the divine orchestration was unfolding exactly as intended. Through Gayton's willingness to be an instrument in God's hands, the ultimate outcome aligned perfectly with the sovereign design of the Creator. Though the ways of the Almighty are often mysterious and inscrutable from a human vantage point, Gayton's story stands as a testament to the truth that when we yield ourselves to the leading of the divine, the plan will always be brought to fruition, even if it does not align with our own limited understanding. In the grand scheme, God has a purpose and a plan, and by entrusting ourselves to that higher calling, we can be assured that the Maker of heaven and earth will work it all out according to His perfect will.

In the face of a seemingly troubling situation, these individuals chose not to intervene, but rather to stand firm in their obedience to God. They understood the profound calling to love one another, recognizing that their own limited human perspectives could never fully comprehend the infinite wisdom and ways of the divine. Indeed, as this passage so eloquently conveys, our minds are not God's mind, nor is our understanding equivalent to His. Time and time again, God provides us with answers to our heartfelt prayers, yet all too often, we fail to recognize the source, hastily rejecting that which does not align with our own preconceived notions. We must remember that the Almighty has a meticulously crafted plan for the world, one that spans the vastness of eternity - from before the very creation of the universe to the glorious second coming of Christ. As the Psalmist so beautifully proclaims, "From everlasting to everlasting, You are God." This is a profound truth we must internalize - that God's sovereign plan encompasses not only the grand sweep of history, but also the intimate details of our individual lives in the present day. If we can learn to humbly submit to His higher ways, trusting in His perfect timing and infinite wisdom, we will discover the profound peace and purpose that comes from aligning our lives with the will of the Almighty.

Driven by a profound sense of purpose and a deep understanding of their role within a greater cosmic tapestry, they embarked on a journey of discovery and transformation. Acutely aware of the interconnectedness of all things, they recognized that their actions held profound implications, reverberating far beyond the confines of their individual experiences. With unwavering conviction, they surrendered to the guiding forces that beckoned them, trusting in the wisdom of a reality that transcended the limits of their mortal comprehension. Every step they took, every decision they made, was imbued with a reverence for the grand design that unfolded before them, a design in which they were but a single thread, woven seamlessly into the intricate tapestry of existence. Through their actions, they sought to align themselves with the rhythms of the universe, becoming conduits for the manifestation of a higher purpose that extended far beyond their own personal desires or ambitions. In this state of heightened awareness and spiritual connection, they moved with a sense of grace and synchronicity, their every deed infused with a profound understanding of their place in the grander scheme of things.

* * *

Three

Chapter 3

In a profound and awe-inspiring moment, the very voice of the divine was heard echoing through the heavens, as God cried out in a thunderous declaration that reverberated across the earth. This was no mere whisper, but a bellowing proclamation that demanded the attention of all who had ears to hear. The Almighty's words were not shrouded in mystery or ambiguity, but rather rang out with a clarity that cut through the noise and confusion of the world, imparting a weighty message that called upon humanity to listen and heed the urgency of the divine summons. It was as if the Creator of all things had parted the veil between the mortal and eternal realms, reaching down to make His presence and will undeniably known. This was no passive, distant deity, but an active, engaged God who sought to commune with His creation, to shake them from their slumber and compel them to align their lives with the eternal truths that emanated from the heavenly throne. In that moment, the very fabric of reality seemed to tremble, for the voice of the Almighty is a force to be reckoned with, carrying with it the weight of absolute power and authority. And so, all who heard this clarion call from on high were left with a profound sense of both awe and responsibility, knowing that they had been granted a rare opportunity to directly hear the voice of the divine and respond accordingly.

In this powerful statement, God makes it clear that His mission is not to judge the righteous, but rather to call the sinners to repentance and salvation. This is a profound and humbling truth - that the Almighty Creator of the universe would stoop down to embrace the lowly, the broken, and the outcast, and offer them the opportunity for redemption. And it is in this spirit that we, as followers of Christ, must heed the call to fight against the scourge of human trafficking that continues to enslave an estimated 40 million people worldwide. These are our brothers and sisters, made in the image of God, who have been cruelly robbed of their freedom and dignity, forced into lives of unimaginable exploitation and abuse. But the light of Christ burns brightly, and we must be His hands and feet, working tirelessly to liberate the captives, to break the chains of their oppressors, and to usher them into the glorious freedom that is their birthright. Let us fall to our knees and plead with the Almighty, the Defender of the weak, to intervene with His mighty power, to shatter the darkness that shrouds this evil industry, and to guide each precious soul into the healing embrace of His love and grace. For if God has not come to call the righteous, but sinners to repentance, then surely His heart burns with a compassion and a fury to see the victims of human trafficking set free - free to know His goodness, free to walk in the light, free to fulfill the purpose for which they were created. Let this be the cry of our souls until the day when the scourge of trafficking is no more.

At the very core of the divine, within the boundless love and wisdom of the Almighty, lies the essence of what it means to truly do what is right. As mortal beings, we are blessed with the gift of free will, the ability to choose our own path and shape our own destiny. Yet, in the face of this profound freedom, we so often find ourselves drawn to the allure of temptation, succumbing to the siren call of our baser impulses rather than heeding the gentle guidance of the divine. When we knowingly turn away from the righteous way, choosing to act in direct opposition to the will of the Lord, we condemn ourselves to the burden of sin. This is the heart of God's lament - not that we are imperfect, for perfection is the realm of the divine, but that we willfully disregard the wisdom and love that flows from the heavens, opting instead to indulge in that which is base and unworthy. It is a tragic irony, for in that moment when we turn our backs on the path of righteousness, we not only betray the trust of our Creator, but we also sever the sacred connection that allows us to truly thrive. The weight of sin is a heavy one to bear, for it separates us from the light and leaves us adrift in the shadows of our own making. Yet, even in our darkest moments, the door to redemption remains open, for the love of God is eternal, and His forgiveness knows no bounds. It is up to us, then, to heed the call, to find the strength to resist temptation and walk the righteous path, that we may once more bask in the radiant glow of the divine heart.

You claim to speak for God, yet you defile the very temples He has created. How dare you presume to understand the sanctity of the human form when you brazenly violate it for your own twisted gain. Each person is a masterpiece, crafted in the divine image, deserving of reverence and protection. But you see only commodities to be bought and sold, stripping away their dignity and worth. You speak of understanding, yet your black heart is void of empathy, deaf to the cries of the innocent you so callously exploit. These are not mere bodies to you, but living, breathing souls - sons, daughters, brothers, sisters - torn from their families, condemned to unspeakable horrors at your cruel hands. And you have the audacity to invoke God's name, as if He would condone such absolute depravity. No, you who traffic in human flesh have forsaken any claim to righteousness. You are an affront to all that is sacred, a cancer upon humanity that must be excised, for until you recognize the divine spark in every person, you can never hope to understand the true meaning of the temple you so brazenly desecrate.

The Bible's message in 1 Corinthians 6:19 is a profound and powerful call for us to recognize the sacred nature of our physical bodies. As followers of Christ, we are told that our bodies are not our own, but rather are "temples of the Holy Spirit" - dwelling places for the very presence of God within us. This means that our physical forms are not merely vessels to be used and exploited as we see fit, but are instead hallowed ground to be treated with the utmost care, reverence, and respect. When we truly internalize this truth, it should dramatically shift our perspective and behavior. If we truly understand that our bodies are not our private property, but are in fact holy sanctuaries consecrated by the indwelling of the divine, then we will be far less inclined to harm, abuse, or defile them through unhealthy, unethical, or immoral actions. Likewise, this realization should compel us to honor our bodies and the bodies of others, regarding them as sacred spaces not to be violated but to be protected, nourished, and treated with the dignity they deserve as God's own temples. This is a challenging and countercultural message in a world that so often reduces the human form to a commodity to be exploited. But for the believer who embraces this biblical principle, it can be a life-changing paradigm shift that imbues every aspect of embodied existence with profound meaning, purpose, and a sense of the divine.

"Do unto others as you would have them do unto you" is a fundamental principle of ethical behavior known as the Golden Rule, which was taught by Jesus Christ in the Gospels of Luke and Matthew. This timeless moral guideline encourages people to treat others with the same kindness, compassion, and respect that they would wish to receive themselves. The concept suggests that we should put ourselves in the shoes of another person and consider how we would want to be treated if we were in their situation. By adopting this perspective, we are motivated to act in a way that is considerate of others' needs and feelings, rather than solely pursuing our own self-interests. The Golden Rule transcends religious and cultural boundaries, as it speaks to the inherent dignity and worth of all human beings. When we live by this principle, we foster an atmosphere of mutual understanding, goodwill, and social harmony. Ultimately, the wisdom of "doing unto others" reminds us of our common humanity and the obligation we have to care for one another, which is a timeless truth that continues to resonate and guide moral conduct across the ages. The concept of the "Golden Rule" is a fundamental principle of ethics and morality that has been espoused by various philosophical and religious traditions throughout history. At its core, the Golden Rule espouses the idea that one should treat others in the way they themselves would wish to be treated. As the biblical passage from the Gospel of Matthew succinctly states, this principle serves as the summation of the Law and the teachings of the Prophets, encapsulating the essence of righteous and virtuous conduct. By encouraging individuals to empathize with and consider the perspectives of others, the Golden Rule promotes compassion, kindness, and a respect for human dignity. It challenges people to move beyond selfish or narcissistic tendencies and instead adopt a mindset of concern for the wellbeing of their fellow human beings. The simplicity and universality of the Golden Rule lend it a timeless appeal, as it provides a clear and accessible ethical guideline that can be applied in myriad personal and social contexts. Whether in one's interactions with family members, friends, strangers, or even adversaries, the Golden Rule beckons us to treat all people with the care, consideration, and civility that we ourselves would hope to receive. In this way, the Golden Rule serves as a touchstone for moral behavior, inspiring individuals to cultivate the better angels of their nature and contribute to the creation of a more harmonious and humane world.

When faced with a choice that logically leads to a less favorable outcome, it can be puzzling why someone would intentionally pursue the opposite path. Yet, this is a tendency that plagues many people, driven by an underlying lack of understanding or insight. The biblical passage from Hosea 4:6 speaks to this issue, warning that "my people are destroyed for lack of knowledge." This lack of knowledge can manifest in various ways - a failure to fully comprehend the consequences of one's actions, an unwillingness to consider the long-term ramifications, or a misguided belief that somehow, against all odds, the unfavorable outcome can be avoided.

Oftentimes, this self-destructive behavior arises from a deep-seated emotional need or compulsion that overrides rational thought. Perhaps there is a lingering resentment or desire for rebellion that leads someone to knowingly choose the worse option, as a form of self-sabotage or passive-aggressive retaliation. Or it could stem from a lack of self-worth, where the individual unconsciously seeks out failure as a way to validate their own feelings of inadequacy. Addictive tendencies can also play a role, where short-term gratification trumps any consideration of the eventual, inevitable pain and suffering.

Ultimately, this pattern of choosing the opposite of what one knows to be the wiser path reflects a fundamental disconnect - a breakdown in the integration of knowledge, wisdom, and self-control. It is a symptom of a deeper spiritual, emotional, or psychological void that the person is struggling to fill. Without addressing the root causes, this self-sabotaging behavior will likely persist, leading to increasingly dire consequences that only further compound the original "lack of knowledge" that set it all in motion. True change requires a willingness to confront one's own limitations, biases, and inner turmoil, in order to realign one's actions with a more enlightened understanding of what is truly in one's best interests.

Far too often, people fall into the trap of overconfidence, believing that they possess a comprehensive understanding of the world around them and the ability to make flawless decisions. This misguided sense of certainty can lead individuals down a dangerous path, as they become blind to their own shortcomings and the complexities that lie beyond their limited perspective. Such hubris is a common ailment, rooted in the innate human desire to feel in control and superior to others. However, this inflated ego frequently clouds one's judgment, causing them to disregard the wisdom and guidance of higher powers, such as the divine teachings of God.

When people succumb to this arrogance, they inevitably find themselves making choices and taking actions that are misguided and ultimately harmful, both to themselves and those around them. Thinking they know better than the omniscient Creator, they disregard the moral and ethical principles laid out in sacred texts, instead prioritizing their own selfish impulses and perceived interests. This willful disobedience to God's laws not only severs the connection to the divine, but also breeds a sense of hubris that blinds the individual to the error of their ways. It is only through humility, self-reflection, and a genuine openness to the teachings of the Almighty that one can hope to overcome this debilitating affliction of overconfidence and find the true path to enlightenment and righteousness.

The insatiable human desire for wealth and material possessions is often the driving force behind the most heinous acts of cruelty and immorality. At the core of this troubling phenomenon is the notion that money can somehow fill the void within us, providing a false sense of fulfillment and contentment. However, as history has repeatedly shown, this belief is fundamentally flawed. The pursuit of riches, no matter how fervent, will never lead to true satisfaction. Instead, it becomes an endless cycle of greed, where one problem merely gives rise to another, an ever-escalating spiral of corruption and callousness.

Those consumed by the love of money often find themselves willing to trample upon the rights and well-being of others, whether through exploitative business practices, callous disregard for the environment, or even outright violence. The single-minded focus on accumulating wealth can cloud moral judgment, eroding empathy and compassion until the only driving force is the unquenchable thirst for more. This warped perspective transforms human beings into soulless automatons, driven by the false promise that material abundance will bring fulfillment.

Tragically, the victims of such avarice are often the most vulnerable members of society - the poor, the marginalized, and the defenseless. As the wealthy and powerful continue to amass their fortunes, they do so at the expense of those who can least afford it, creating a deeply unjust and imbalanced world. This vicious cycle perpetuates itself, with the disparity between the haves and the have-nots growing ever wider, fueling further resentment and the potential for even greater acts of cruelty.

Ultimately, the root cause of such abhorrent behavior lies in the human tendency to confuse wealth with worth, to believe that the accumulation of material possessions can somehow fill the void within. But as countless cautionary tales have shown, this is a hollow and destructive path, one that leads only to more problems, more suffering, and a profound lack of true, lasting happiness. Only by recognizing the inherent limitations of money and the true sources of fulfillment - compassion, empathy, and a sense of purpose beyond the self - can we hope to break this vicious cycle and create a more just and humane world.

The tragic reality is that children often find themselves in grave danger, facing the terrifying prospect of getting lost, being abducted, or even losing their lives. And sadly, these heartbreaking incidents are all too frequently driven by the most base of human motivations - greed, addiction, and malice. When money and drugs become the driving forces behind someone's actions, the sanctity of human life, especially that of the most vulnerable, is callously disregarded. Twisted individuals who would stoop to harming a child often seem to have a complete disconnect from the concept of family and the profound love that should accompany it. How can a parent, sibling, or other loved one bring themselves to inflict such trauma, when they themselves have surely experienced the unconditional bond of kinship? Yet the painful truth is that familial ties provide no safeguard - those who commit these heinous acts are all too often family members or acquaintances, people who should be protectors but instead become predators. The loss, the violation of trust, the irreparable damage done - it is a cycle of tragedy that repeats itself far too often, one problem leading to another in a devastating spiral. If only those who would harm the innocent could pause and remember the precious lives they hold in their hands, the cherished loved ones in their own lives - maybe then they would resist the dark impulses that drive them to commit such unspeakable acts.

It's a profound and troubling question that has puzzled many - how can individuals who commit heinous acts of violence or cruelty seemingly lack any empathy or consideration for their own loved ones? The notion that someone could inflict such harm on another human being, without any apparent concern for how they themselves would feel if the roles were reversed, is deeply unsettling. One can't help but wonder, do these perpetrators truly not have family or close relationships of their own? Have they never experienced the unconditional love, comfort and support that comes from having people who care deeply about your wellbeing? Or is it perhaps that in their minds, the victims they target are somehow less deserving of that same compassion - that they have dehumanized or disconnected from the reality that their targets are also someone's child, parent, partner or friend? It's a disturbing psychological disconnect that is difficult to fathom. Perhaps they have become so consumed by their own anger, pain or twisted motives that the humanity of their victims becomes obscured. Or maybe they have simply lost the ability to empathize, to put themselves in another's shoes and recognize the true scope of the suffering they are inflicting. Whatever the root cause, the lack of remorse or consideration for how their actions would impact their own loved ones is truly chilling. It's a question that gets to the heart of the human capacity for cruelty, and one that continues to haunt and perplex us.

In God's eyes, it is never acceptable or justifiable to inflict harm upon another human being. This goes against the very essence of what God wants us to be and do for one another. The divine commandment to love thy neighbor as thyself is a core tenet of most major religions, yet far too often, people choose to disregard this sacred calling in pursuit of more earthly, material desires. The love of money, in particular, has a corrupting influence that can lead individuals down a dark path of greed, selfishness, and cruelty. When the quest for wealth and possessions becomes the primary driving force in one's life, it inevitably requires stepping on the backs of others, exploiting their vulnerabilities, and treating them as means to an end rather than as precious children of God. This is the very definition of evil - the willful disregard for the inherent dignity and worth of another person, all for the sake of personal gain. God desires that we see the divine spark in each and every human life, and respond with compassion, generosity, and a commitment to the common good. To do otherwise, to willfully harm another under the sway of mammon, is to utterly betray the sacred trust that has been placed in us. It is a perversion of our God-given purpose and a grave sin against both our fellow man and the Almighty. Only by aligning our hearts and actions with God's will of love and justice can we hope to fulfill our true calling as children of the Divine.

The sudden and unexplained disappearance of children and all human life is a truly chilling and unsettling phenomenon that has gripped communities around the world. In some cases, these vanishings appear to be driven by darker, more sinister motives - acts of revenge, hatred, and pure spitefulness. Entire families can vanish without a trace, leaving behind only confusion, grief, and unanswered questions. Investigators struggle to uncover the truth, with few clues or witnesses to guide them. Some theorize that these disappearances are orchestrated by shadowy figures harboring deep-seated resentments, seeking to inflict maximum pain and suffering on innocent victims. Others speculate that supernatural or extraterrestrial forces may be at play, whisking people away to unknown realms beyond our comprehension. Whatever the cause, the emotional toll on those left behind is immense, as they are forced to grapple with the unbearable uncertainty of not knowing the fate of their loved ones. In the void left by these unexplained vanishings, mistrust, fear, and paranoia can take root, as communities struggle to make sense of the senseless. The disappearance of children, in particular, strikes at the very heart of human compassion, leaving an indelible mark of trauma that may never fully heal. As the search continues for answers and closure, the specter of these unsettling events continues to haunt the collective consciousness, a stark reminder of the fragility of our existence and the darkness that can lurk in the shadows of the human experience. The call of the Last Supper has echoed through the ages, a timeless message that continues to resonate with us even in the present day. In the modern world, we see its influence manifested in unexpected ways, such as the mysterious disappearance of Joslin Smith. This tragic event, along with countless others like it, serves as a sobering reminder that the divine call to fellowship and understanding, as exemplified by Christ's final meal with his disciples, has not been heeded as it should. Through these unsettling occurrences, we are confronted with the stark reality that humanity has often fallen short of the compassion and unity embodied in that sacred gathering. Yet, the persistent call remains, urging us to heed the lessons of the past and strive for a world where the spirit of the Last Supper - one of forgiveness, solidarity, and unwavering faith - guides our actions. It is a summons that transcends time and space, challenging us to look beyond the veil of our own self-interests and answer the divine plea for a more just, harmonious existence. For in the eyes of the Almighty, enough is indeed enough - a clarion call to reclaim the timeless wisdom that has been passed down to us, and to finally live up to the profound legacy of that fateful, final supper.

The omnipotent, all-knowing God is urgently calling out to each and every one of us in a thunderous, booming voice that cannot be ignored. He is imploring us, His beloved children, to cease our harmful actions and behaviors that are contributing to the steady decline and deterioration of our precious world. God sees with His divine, all-seeing eyes the countless ways in which humanity has strayed from His righteous path - the rampant greed, the senseless violence, the wanton disregard for the delicate balance of nature. He grieves as He watches us destroy the very planet He so lovingly created and entrusted to our care. In a voice that resonates with a mix of sorrow, frustration, and unwavering authority, the Almighty is beseeching us to stop - to stop the exploitation, the oppression, the reckless pillaging of the Earth's finite resources. He yearns for us to open our hearts and truly listen, to heed His urgent pleas before it is too late to reverse the irreparable damage we have wrought. God's message is clear - it is time for humanity to have a profound reckoning, to make the necessary changes to our thoughts, our priorities, our actions, in order to be good stewards of this world and ensure a brighter, more sustainable future for generations to come. The choice is ours, but the clock is ticking, and the Heavenly Father's cries grow ever more insistent.

In this critical moment, the Almighty Lord of Hosts delivers a profound and urgent message to His people. He calls upon them to purify themselves, to cleanse their hearts and minds of all that is unrighteous and impure. The Lord demands that they cast away their wicked deeds, removing them from His sight, for He can no longer look upon such transgressions. It is time, He declares, to cease from all evil, to turn away from the temptations and snares that have led them astray. This is a moment of reckoning, a time for deep introspection and repentance. The Lord implores His flock to heed His words, to humble themselves before Him, and to seek the path of righteousness once more. For only by washing themselves clean, by rooting out the corruption within, can they hope to find favor in the eyes of the Almighty and be spared from the consequences of their misdeeds. This clarion call is a testament to God's enduring love, but also to His righteous indignation at the transgressions of His people. It is a message that demands action, a summons to turn away from the darkness and embrace the light of divine grace. In heeding this urgent directive, the faithful may find redemption and the restoration of their sacred covenant with the Lord of Hosts. Jealousy is a toxic emotion that can poison even the closest of relationships. Instead, we must strive to cultivate a spirit of love and compassion towards one another. When we let go of the green-eyed monster of envy, we open ourselves up to truly seeing and appreciating the unique gifts and talents of those around us. Rather than resenting their successes or comparing ourselves to them, we can celebrate their achievements and honor the inherent worth and dignity in each person. This is the way of wisdom and grace. And it is not always easy - the human heart is prone to covetousness and self-absorption. But we must remember that our lives are not a zero-sum game. Another person's blessing does not diminish our own. In fact, by freely giving one another the respect, admiration and encouragement they deserve, we all stand to benefit. For even before we drew our first breath, the Almighty had a perfect plan in place for each of our lives. Our value is not contingent on how we measure up to our peers, but is rooted in the unconditional love of our Creator. When we internalize this truth, jealousy and comparison fall away, and we are liberated to live in harmony, celebrating one another's successes as our own. This is the beautiful tapestry that emerges when we choose to walk the path of selfless love.

* * *

Four

Chapter 4

To those responsible for the disappearance of innocent people, your actions are utterly abhorrent and unjustifiable, not only in the eyes of society but in the eyes of a higher moral authority as well. What you have done is an egregious violation of human rights and the sanctity of life itself. You have torn families apart, left loved ones in anguish, and robbed individuals of their freedom and their futures. The guilt and shame you must feel, cowering in the shadows of your own twisted machinations, is a testament to the depravity of your deeds. That guilt should haunt you, weighing heavily upon your conscience and permeating every aspect of your existence. You may try to hide from the world, to evade justice and accountability, but the specter of your misdeeds will forever loom over you. There is no escape from the moral reckoning you so richly deserve. The lives you have destroyed, the pain you have inflicted - these are sins that can never be absolved, not in the eyes of your fellow humans nor in the judgment of a higher divine power. The cage in which you find yourself trapped is of your own making, a prison constructed by the weight of your own transgressions. Until you muster the courage to face the enormity of your actions and seek atonement, that cage will only grow smaller, the walls closing in as the reality of your guilt consumes you. The time has come for you to emerge from the shadows, to confront the consequences of your choices, and to reckon with the moral reckoning that awaits.

This is not merely a message of one's own making, but rather the profound proclamation of the divine Creator who breathed life into all things. As we grapple with the challenges and consequences of our own actions, it is natural to wonder how we might find a path to resolution. The problems we have created, the damage we have wrought - these weigh heavily upon our conscience, leaving us to ponder how we can possibly make amends. Yet, in this moment of self-reflection, we must heed the wisdom that transcends our own limited understanding. For the one who fashioned the very fabric of existence holds the keys to restoration and redemption. Though our missteps may have carved deep grooves in the landscape of our lives, the message of the Almighty offers hope - a invitation to align ourselves with a higher purpose, to seek forgiveness, and to engage in the sacred work of repairing what we have broken. This is no simple task, but one that requires humility, courage, and a willingness to surrender our own agenda in service of a grander design. As we heed this call, we may find that the very challenges we once saw as insurmountable become the pathways to our own spiritual growth and the healing of our world. For the message of the Creator is not one of condemnation, but of boundless compassion - a summons to rise above our limitations and become vessels of transformation, restoring harmony where discord once reigned supreme. While it may feel like the weight of the world is on your shoulders, there is indeed some good news for you as well. Though you may have made a misstep or two, or even strayed down the wrong path for a time, the important thing is that you are willing to acknowledge your mistake and make the choice to change direction. We are all human, after all, and none of us are perfect - we all falter and stumble at times, giving in to temptation or poor judgment. But the true test of one's character lies not in the mistakes themselves, but in how we respond to them. By taking responsibility for your actions and resolving to learn from this experience, you demonstrate the strength and integrity that will allow you to move forward in a more positive way. This is not the end, but rather an opportunity for growth and renewal. Though the road ahead may seem daunting, know that you are not alone, and that with the right mindset and determination, you can absolutely get your life back on track. No one is written off or beyond redemption - we all have the capacity within us to acknowledge our faults, make amends, and find the right path once more. This is your chance to do just that, to prove your resilience and emerge from this chapter of your life as a wiser, more grounded individual. The way forward may not be easy, but it is there for the taking, if you are willing to take that first brave step.

It's a common sentiment, the idea that while no one else may be judging us, God is always watching and evaluating our actions. This notion of divine judgment can weigh heavily on the conscience, serving as a constant reminder to live a righteous and moral life. Yet, the message conveyed here goes beyond simply being mindful of God's omniscient gaze. It suggests a call to action - to stop whatever it is we are currently occupied with and re-evaluate our priorities and behaviors. The reference to the Joslin's Smith matter of disappearance adds a sense of urgency and gravity to this exhortation, hinting that there may be unseen forces or consequences at play that demand our immediate attention and obedience. By pausing whatever tasks or diversions we have immersed ourselves in, we open ourselves up to deeper spiritual reflection and the possibility of divine guidance. It's a sobering yet empowering message - that we need not fear the judgment of our fellow man, for it is only the judgment of God that truly matters in the grand scheme of our lives. In heeding this advice to cease our current activities and surrender to a higher power, we may find clarity, purpose, and the strength to live more intentionally in alignment with our faith. This is a weighty charge, but one that could profoundly transform our perspective and redirect the course of our lives if taken to heart.

The news that Joslin may have been the victim of a horrific practice called muti was truly devastating to hear. Muti is a term used to describe the use of human body parts, often obtained through murder or grave robbery, in traditional African medicine and rituals. The very idea that someone could have been killed and mutilated for such a purpose is utterly abhorrent and heartbreaking. It speaks to a profound darkness and disregard for human life that is difficult to fathom. In a world where people should be treating each other with dignity and compassion, the thought that anyone could commit such an evil act is simply incomprehensible.

While it's true that not everyone shares the same religious or spiritual beliefs, the fundamental principles of kindness, empathy and respect for others should transcend any particular faith or worldview. To knowingly cause harm to another person, to use them as an object for one's own gain or ritual, is a grave violation of our common humanity. We must ask ourselves - is a belief system that promotes cruelty, that fails to value human life, truly righteous or justified? Shouldn't our deepest convictions compel us to love our fellow human beings, to protect the vulnerable, and to uplift our shared dignity? The tragic case of Joslin serves as a sobering reminder that we all have a moral obligation to stand against the forces of darkness, hatred and violence, and to instead cultivate a world defined by compassion, empathy and the sacred worth of every person. Only then can we begin to heal the brokenness that weighs so heavily on the human heart.

Despite the initial suspicion that Joslin might have been involved in something as sinister as muti practices, the I, still maintains a sense of hope that she will somehow emerge from whatever circumstances she finds herself in. There is an underlying belief that the truth will eventually come to light, even if it takes time. I, expresses a conviction that those responsible for any wrongdoing or harm that has befallen Joslin will ultimately face judgment for their actions.

This hopefulness is coupled with a deeper philosophical query about the nature of love. I ponders where love can be found within one's own heart, positing that the answer may lie in the very beliefs and values that guide one's life.

There is an implication that true love transcends surface-level assumptions or prejudices. I asserts that it is inherently wrong to withhold love from another person, as well as to treat fellow human beings with the same callousness one might treat an animal. These sentiments suggest a moral stance rooted in compassion, empathy and the fundamental dignity of all people. When one's beliefs or worldview are grounded in a lack of love, rather than embracing love, it is a deeply problematic and concerning state of being. The opposite of love is not simply indifference or apathy, but rather, the toxic and corrosive emotion of hatred. To hold beliefs that are fundamentally rooted in hatred towards others is a profoundly misguided and morally bankrupt position. Hatred, at its core, is an evil force that breeds only more hatred, division, and suffering in the world. It is the antithesis of the compassion, empathy, and universal human connection that love represents.

When an individual's belief system is built upon a foundation of hate, it poisons their entire outlook and relationship to the world around them. They see others not as fellow human beings worthy of dignity and respect,

The passage from Leviticus 19:17 in the Bible provides profound guidance on how we should approach our relationships with others. It speaks to the importance of not harboring hatred or resentment in our hearts, even towards those who may have wronged us. The text instructs us to confront such feelings head-on, not allowing them to fester and poison our interactions. By addressing issues directly and honestly with our neighbors, we avoid becoming complicit in their misdeeds. This underscores a core tenet of ethical living - that we have a responsibility to call out injustice and hold each other accountable, but to do so through open and thoughtful dialogue, rather than through bottled-up anger or passive-aggressive behaviors. The wisdom of this passage recognizes our common humanity, and the reality that we all make mistakes. Rather than cutting ourselves off from those who have erred, we are called to engage with them, to understand their perspectives, and to guide them back towards righteous actions. In this way, we strengthen the bonds of community and avoid the spiritual and social decay that festers when hatred is allowed to take root. Heeding the lesson of Leviticus 19:17 is thus a powerful means of cultivating a more just, compassionate, and unified world.

The sentiment that we must not hate but instead learn to love and live in peace is a profound and vital truth that we would do well to heed. At the core of this principle is the recognition that hatred and division only breed more negativity and suffering, while love and compassion have the power to transform the world around us. When we prioritize material wealth and worldly possessions over our connection to the divine, our higher purpose becomes obscured, and we can easily fall into the trap of greed, selfishness, and malice. This misguided focus causes us to turn against one another, lashing out in anger and resentment rather than extending empathy and understanding. Yet the antidote to this cycle of hate lies in cultivating a genuine love - for our Creator, for our fellow human beings, and for the sacred tapestry of life that binds us all together. By shifting our priorities and aligning our hearts with the higher virtues of kindness, forgiveness, and harmony, we open ourselves up to a profound transformation, one that allows us to see the inherent dignity and worth in every person, regardless of their station or circumstance. It is only through this radical embrace of love that we can hope to transcend the petty divisions and conflicts that so often plague our world, and instead build a society founded on the timeless principles of peace, justice, and mutual respect. Though the path may not always be easy, the rewards of this journey are immeasurable, for in learning to love unconditionally, we unlock the door to a more enlightened and fulfilling existence, both for ourselves and for all of humanity.

During a time of personal struggle and turmoil, Joslin felt a profound spiritual connection as God imparted a specific scripture to them. In that moment, Joslin could palpably sense the intensity of God's emotions - an underlying current of righteous anger, yet tempered by an enduring, unconditional love for all of humanity. Though the world had fallen into darkness and discord, provoking the Almighty's wrath, there remained a glimmer of mercy and compassion within the divine heart. God, in His infinite wisdom and patience, sought to guide Joslin through this turbulent period, imparting wisdom and perspective even as He wrestled with the temptation to unleash His full judgment upon the wayward souls populating the earth. It was a humbling, awe-inspiring experience for Joslin, to bear witness to the complex tapestry of divine emotions - the passionate fury juxtaposed with the steadfast, merciful love that lies at the very core of God's nature. In that sacred moment, Joslin was granted a rare glimpse into the profound internal struggle within the Almighty as He wrestled to maintain control, to withhold the full weight of His wrath, in order to preserve the possibility of redemption for a world that had strayed so far from His intended path. It was a profoundly moving and enlightening encounter that left an indelible mark on Joslin's soul.

As a devout believer, the anguish of losing young Joslin, we all cherished "little green-eyed angel," weighed heavily on the peoples of Saldahna buy's heart.

Night after night, they had poured out their souls in fervent prayer, begging God to grant them the wisdom, power, strength, knowledge, and profound understanding they so desperately needed to make sense of this unimaginable tragedy. How could such a vibrant, beloved child simply vanish from the earth without a trace? It was a mystery that defied all logic and reason, leaving the family and their entire faith community reeling. Yet, in the depths of their grief, they clung to the belief that the Almighty had a purpose, a message He was trying to impart - if only they could discern His will. Perhaps there were lessons to be learned, a higher plan unfolding that was beyond their mortal comprehension. Though the pain was excruciating, they remained steadfast in their faith, trusting that God would find a way to reach them, to provide the answers and comfort they so ardently sought. In their darkest hour, this family of believers knew they must continue seeking divine guidance, open and receptive to whatever profound revelation the Lord had in store - for only then could they begin to heal and find peace, despite the overwhelming loss of their cherished Joslin.

The situation described was undoubtedly a heartbreaking one that resonated deeply with the church community as a whole. When faced with such profound injustice and cruelty, it was only natural that the faithful would feel compelled to raise their voices and take a stand for what they knew to be righteous in the eyes of God. The biblical passage from Exodus 21:16 in particular seemed to offer a clear condemnation of the abhorrent practice of trafficking or kidnapping free people and then selling them into slavery - a direct violation of the divine commandments. This scripture struck a powerful chord, galvanizing the church to speak up boldly against such grave moral transgressions. The gravity of the circumstances demanded a forceful response, one that would make it unequivocally clear that the exploitation and dehumanization of any of God's children was wholly unacceptable and flew in the face of the compassionate, justice-oriented teachings at the heart of the faith. In the midst of this heartbreaking situation, the unwavering conviction of the church to uphold the sacred principles of human dignity and freedom provided a beacon of hope, inspiring the community to unite in their righteous crusade against the evils of slavery and human trafficking. Through their impassioned advocacy and appeals to the higher moral authority, the church sought to ensure that justice would ultimately prevail, no matter the odds.

Faced with the daunting uncertainty of her circumstances, the young little girl, might have found herself in a truly heartbreaking predicament. With no clear sense of where she might end up next, the prospect of securing a proper, nourishing meal seemed to grow more and more elusive with each passing moment. The gnawing pangs of hunger only compounded the distress and anxiety she felt, as she struggled to imagine how she would manage to find sustenance in her precarious situation. Each time she contemplated her dire circumstances, a deep, aching sadness would well up within her, a profound empathy for her own plight that threatened to overwhelm her. It was a profoundly unsettling state of affairs, this not knowing where her next meal might come from, this lack of stability and security that left her feeling profoundly adrift and alone. Though she tried to maintain hope, the sheer weight of her circumstances threatened to crush her spirit, leaving her to confront the harsh reality that even the most basic of human needs - During this pivotal time, the divine presence and wisdom of God was revealed with remarkable clarity, serving as a profound call to humanity. As we reflect on this sacred period, it becomes abundantly clear that we must approach God's word with the utmost seriousness and sincerity, allowing it to penetrate deeply into our hearts and minds. For the Almighty Lord never retracts or wavers in the eternal truths He has imparted to us through His divine revelations. These timeless teachings are not mere suggestions or fleeting advice, but rather immutable principles that have the power to transform our lives if only we have the courage to embrace them fully.

In a world often filled with uncertainty and shifting priorities, God's word stands as an unwavering beacon, guiding us towards a deeper understanding of our purpose and the divine plan for our existence. To treat these sacred scriptures and commandments with anything less than the reverence they deserve would be to risk losing sight of the transcendent wisdom they contain. It is incumbent upon us, as God's children, to approach this divine knowledge with humility, diligence, and an open heart, for it is only through such earnest engagement that we can hope to unlock the profound truths that will lead us to a more fulfilling and purposeful life. The clarity of God's message during this pivotal time is a testament to His eternal commitment to our spiritual growth and well-being, and it is our sacred duty to respond with the utmost dedication and obedience.

The topic of punishing those involved in the abhorrent act of human trafficking is a grave and serious matter that demands our utmost attention and condemnation. The harsh penalty of death imposed on anyone found guilty of stealing a person and selling them into slavery reflects the utter depravity and cruelty of such a heinous crime. These individuals rob their victims of the most fundamental human rights - the freedom to live autonomous lives, to make their own choices, and to maintain their inherent dignity. By treating fellow human beings as mere commodities to be bought and sold, traffickers demonstrate a complete disregard for the sanctity of life and the inviolable principles of personal liberty. The severity of the prescribed punishment underscores just how abhorrent this practice is viewed by society, as it rightly seeks to stamp out such egregious exploitation and abuse through the most severe legal consequences. No person should ever have to endure the trauma of being ripped from their life and forced into servitude against their will. This uncompromising stance sends a clear message that a civilized, moral society will not tolerate the buying and selling of human beings under any circumstances, and that those who engage in such despicable acts will be met with the harshest possible retribution. The weight of this crime is so grave that only the ultimate penalty can truly reflect the magnitude of the offense and provide justice for the victims and their loved ones whose lives have been irrevocably shattered.

When God speaks, His words hold the power to transform the world. As the omniscient Creator, He sees the full scope of history and the destiny of all humanity. So when God declares something, it is not mere speculation or a vague suggestion - it is a promise that will undoubtedly come to pass. His utterances carry the weight of absolute truth and divine authority. Throughout the scriptures, we see countless examples of God's prophetic words manifesting exactly as He foretold, whether it was the deliverance of the Israelites from Egypt, the rise and fall of great kingdoms, or the coming of the Messiah. Even when His warnings seem dire or His commands seem challenging, we can trust that they are spoken for our ultimate good, to guide us towards His perfect plan. As the Almighty, God is not constrained by human timelines or limited by our understanding. He works according to His sovereign will and in His perfect timing, ensuring that every word He speaks finds its ultimate fulfillment. In this way, God graciously provides advance notice of what is to come, giving us the opportunity to heed His voice, align our lives with His purposes, and be prepared for the unfolding of His divine blueprint for the world. His prophetic utterances are not mere predictions, but divine declarations that will surely come to pass, reminding us of His omnipotence, faithfulness, and loving care for His people.

The eternal, immutable nature of God's word is a profound and comforting truth for believers. As the passage from 1 Peter states, the word of the Lord remains forever - it is not fleeting or temporary, but endures for all eternity. This word, which refers to the gospel message that has been preached and shared, is the very foundation upon which our faith is built. Unlike the temporal, ever-changing world around us, God's word stands firm and unshakable, a solid rock upon which we can anchor our lives. When all else fades and crumbles, the truth of Scripture persists, a beacon guiding us through the storms of life. This is the remarkable power and permanence of the divine word - it transcends the limits of human existence, outlasting empires and generations, for it originates from the eternal, unchanging God Himself. No matter how much the world may shift and evolve, believers can take solace in knowing that the good news of salvation, as revealed in Scripture, will remain steadfast and secure forever. It is this unwavering constancy of God's word that strengthens our faith, comforts our hearts, and assures us of His eternal promises. In a world of flux and uncertainty, the permanence of the Lord's word provides a steady foundation that will never be shaken.

Humankind's fundamental disobedience to the divine commands and will of God is a central theme that carries immense weight and consequence throughout the human experience. At the core, we as a species have an innate tendency to stray from the righteous path laid out for us, succumbing instead to our baser impulses and selfish desires. This willful defiance of God's teachings and authority has played out time and time again, with disastrous results that reverberate through the ages. When people turn away from the guidance and wisdom of the Almighty, they invite calamity, suffering, and the erosion of the social and moral fabric that is meant to uphold a just, harmonious society. As this book will later explore in depth, the dire consequences of such widespread disobedience have manifested in specific ways within this country, as citizens have cast aside their reverence for the divine commandments and pursued their own misguided agendas. The resulting unrest, conflict, and societal breakdown serve as a sobering reminder that humankind ignores God's will at our own peril, and that true peace, prosperity, and fulfillment can only be achieved through humble obedience and a steadfast commitment to the eternal truths laid out for us. Only by rediscovering our reverence for the divine and aligning our actions with God's vision for humanity can we hope to overcome the cycles of disobedience that have plagued us throughout history.

During my time spent in prayer and contemplation, seeking answers from God regarding the mysterious disappearance of our dear own flesh and blood and community member, Joslin, I've come to a deeper understanding of the profound significance behind this event.

Joslin, I believe, was hand-picked by the divine for a purpose greater than we can fully comprehend in this moment. Though the loss of one so cherished has undoubtedly left an aching void in our hearts and our congregation, we must trust that there is a higher plan unfolding, one that extends far beyond the limits of our human perspective.

In times of darkness and uncertainty such as this, the church is called to be a beacon of hope, a sanctuary where we can collectively grieve, support one another, and draw strength from our unwavering faith. For Joslin was not merely one of us, but a child of God, chosen to fulfill a sacred role in this unfolding divine narrative. Though we may never know the full extent of Joslin's purpose on this earth, we can take solace in the knowledge that her light continues to shine, guiding us towards a deeper understanding of the mysteries that lie at the very core of our shared humanity. Joslin's memory will forever be etched into the fabric of our communities, a testament to the profound impact one life can have, even in its absence.

Let us honor her legacy by standing firm in our faith, supporting one another, and trusting that even in the darkest of times, God's plan will prevail.

The book's title, "The Last Supper," is a poignant and evocative reference to the final meal Jesus shared with his disciples before his crucifixion. For centuries, this sacred moment has held deep significance for followers of Christ, who gather regularly to partake in a ritual reenactment of that fateful night. Known variously as the Lord's Supper, Communion, or the Eucharist, this solemn observance derives its name from the Greek word eucharisteo, meaning "to give thanks." In this profoundly symbolic act, believers come together to commemorate Jesus' selfless sacrifice and to receive the spiritual nourishment of his body and blood, represented by the bread and wine. The solemnity of the occasion is palpable, as participants reflect on the gravity of Christ's impending passion and death, which would irrevocably transform the course of human history. Yet, even in the shadow of the cross, there is an undercurrent of hope and thanksgiving, for it is in this final meal that Jesus establishes the new covenant, promising eternal life to all who put their faith in him. Thus, the "Last Supper" serves as a poignant and powerful reminder of the love, grace, and redemption at the heart of the Christian faith, inspiring believers to approach this sacred rite with reverence, gratitude, and a renewed commitment to follow in the footsteps of their Savior.

You know why I called this book the The Last suppers call?

Because Joslin came by God's call to expose so many things.

The tragic disappearance of Joslin' Smith has become a pivotal moment in the fight against the scourge of child trafficking and dark occult practices. This innocent child, whose very existence was previously unknown to most, has now become a powerful symbol of the immense suffering endured by countless vulnerable youth. Her sacrifice, though unimaginably painful, has shone a light into the shadows where these unspeakable crimes have long festered.

Through her disappearance, the true horrors of human trafficking have been exposed, galvanizing the public and authorities alike to take decisive action.

No longer will missing children be reduced to mere case files, quickly forgotten.

This girl's story has ensured that every vanished youth will now be pursued relentlessly, with the full weight of the law and community outrage behind the efforts to locate them and bring their abusers to justice.

Furthermore, the girl's tragic fate has unveiled the dark underbelly of occult practices that have operated in the shadows, using innocent lives as offerings at twisted altars. These devilish rites, long hidden from public view, have now been dragged into the light, their practitioners exposed and their unholy sanctuaries destroyed. The community, once paralyzed by fear, has risen up to reclaim their streets, their neighborhoods, their very souls, from the grip of this malevolent evil.

Through unimaginable pain and loss, this young life has become a clarion call - a demand that the cycle of missing children and unspeakable crimes must end. And so, in the wake of this tragedy, God's grace and justice have begun to unfold, setting in motion a profound transformation that will safeguard the vulnerable and shine the light of truth into the darkest corners of the world.

The Lord's Supper is far more than just a religious ritual or ceremony - it is a profound invitation into the very heart of the Christian life. The roots of this sacred meal stretch all the way back to the earliest pages of the biblical narrative, where we find God's original design for humanity's relationship with Him. In the Garden of Eden, the Creator walked and fellowshipped directly with the first man and woman, sharing meals and intimate communion. But sin severed that perfect connection, leaving a gaping chasm between God and His beloved creation. Yet even in humanity's darkest hour, God began to lay the groundwork for restoration, hinting at a future feast where the divide would be bridged once more. From the Passover lamb sacrificed to spare the Israelites in Egypt, to the manna raining down from heaven to nourish the people in the wilderness, God consistently used meals and food to point forward to an ultimate reconciliation. And then, in the fullness of time, Jesus Christ - the very Son of God - took bread and wine and declared them to be His own body and blood, a new covenant sealed in His sacrificial death. In this simple yet profound act, the Lord invited His followers into an intimate, ongoing relationship, a life-giving communion where they could encounter His presence, receive His sustenance, and participate in the restoration of all things. Far more than just an obligatory ritual, the Lord's Supper is a beautiful, hope-filled invitation to the wedding feast of the Lamb, a foretaste of the day when God will once again dwell with man, and we will eat and drink in His eternal, unbroken company.

The disappearance of Joslin was a watershed moment that unlocked a wealth of understanding and gratitude. Though the circumstances surrounding her vanishing were shrouded in mystery and heartbreak, the aftermath of this tragic event shed light on the profound sacrifices she had made, and the pivotal role she had played in the lives of those around her. As the community grappled with the sudden void left by Joslin's absence, they were forced to confront the true measure of her impact – the selfless acts of kindness, the quiet moments of support, the unwavering strength that had so often gone unnoticed and unappreciated. It was only through this profound loss that the full extent of Joslin's contributions became clear, sparking a groundswell of thankfulness for the burdens she had borne and the trials she had endured on behalf of her loved ones. In the wake of her disappearance, the community rallied together, united in their desire to honor Joslin's memory and carry forward the legacy of compassion and resilience that she had embodied. The gratitude they expressed was not merely a fleeting sentiment, but a deep and abiding recognition of the sacrifices that true heroes make – the willingness to step into the shadows, to shoulder the weight of others' struggles, to put the needs of the many before the needs of the self. And so, in the absence of Joslin's physical presence, her spirit lived on, a guiding light that inspired those she had left behind to cherish the gift of her life and the profound impact of her unwavering dedication.

As the details of the young girl's ordeal slowly came to light, a complex and heartbreaking story began to emerge. One could only imagine the terror and confusion she must have felt, torn from the safety and comfort of her own home, her mother's betrayal a painful wound that cut deeper than any physical harm. Did she have the chance to eat or drink during her captivity, or was the fear of her situation too overwhelming to even contemplate such basic needs? And what of the longing for her mother - the same woman who, driven by the demons of addiction, had callously sold her own flesh and blood for the means to feed her dependency? It was a level of betrayal almost too difficult to fathom. What unseen traumas and pressures had led the mother down such a dark path, and what became of her once authorities intervened? For the young girl, the road to recovery would undoubtedly be long and arduous, the scars of this ordeal etched into her psyche, perhaps never to fully heal. This was no simple tale of abduction, but a complex web of despair, addiction, and the horrific consequences when the unconditional love of a parent is so tragically, irrevocably broken.

The belief that God has prepared a special, nourishing meal for those enduring great suffering and hardship is a profound and comforting one. The idea suggests that even in our darkest moments, when we feel utterly alone and overwhelmed, the divine presence is there to sustain and strengthen us. Just as a loving parent might tenderly feed a sick child, the divine spirit is envisioned as gently offering spiritual sustenance to those in the throes of anguish and despair. This metaphorical "first meal" provided by God harkens back to the very origins of humanity, when in the first pages of Genesis, the Creator invited the first man and woman to partake in the abundance of the natural world. It is a reminder that even amidst the most trying of circumstances, we are never truly abandoned, for a heavenly table has been set before us, offering nourishment not just for the body, but for the weary soul. Though the mother in this story was consumed by the inner demons plaguing her mind, her daughter was granted the divine privilege of eating from the hands of the Spirit itself, a tangible symbol of God's unwavering care and provision. In this way, the concept of the "special meal" prepared by the divine.

In the biblical account of creation, God appoints humanity

to be his representatives on earth, entrusting them with the profound responsibility of using their own creative power and imagination to spread the order, beauty, and flourishing of the garden-temple to the rest of the untamed creation. This garden where humanity is first placed is a verdant, life-giving paradise, teeming with lush vegetation and abundant resources. Trees laden with succulent, nourishing fruit dot the landscape, ready to be cultivated and enjoyed by the human caretakers. Yet at the very center of this idyllic garden stands a tree of unparalleled significance - the tree of life. This mystical, symbolic tree represents God's ultimate gift to his creation: the opportunity to share in and receive the divine life and vitality that flows from the Creator himself. By granting unfettered access to this life-giving tree, God invites the first man and woman to partake of his own eternal nature, to bask in the fullness of his presence, and to carry that sacred life-force out into the world as his image-bearers and co-creators. The tree of life, then, becomes a tangible symbol of humanity's high calling - to steward the wonders of the garden, to cultivate its bounty, and to expand the borders of God's resplendent kingdom throughout all the earth. With this lofty commission, the first humans are entrusted with an unparalleled privilege, one that calls them to exercise their God-given creativity and imagination in service of the divine plan for all of creation.

The proximity to the tree of life represents a profound, intimate connection to the very source of all existence – the author of life Himself. This tree, so central to the biblical narrative, is not merely a symbolic or metaphorical construct, but a tangible, life-giving entity meant for humanity to directly partake of and consume. In the Genesis account, God's first command to the newly created man and woman is an open invitation to freely eat from all the trees in the garden, including this tree of life – a remarkable offer to ingest the very essence of the divine, to take God's own life-force into one's being. This transformative meal was intended to imbue the partaker with the gift of eternal life, transcending the mortal limitations of the physical form. To dwell in proximity to this tree, then, was to exist in the closest possible communion with the author of all creation, to stand at the wellspring of unending vitality and existence. It represented a state of perfect harmony and intimacy with the divine, where the created and the creator coexisted in a seamless, life-sustaining relationship. This tree, so central to the human story, encapsulates the profound truth that we are not merely passive observers in the grand scheme, but intended to be active participants in the very life of God – to literally ingest and be nourished by the essence of our maker, and thus be transformed and elevated to a plane of eternal being.

The divine invitation to partake in God's eternal feast is one that humanity so often rejects, despite the profound wisdom and nourishment it offers. This sacred meal, prepared with the utmost care and love by the Creator himself, represents the very essence of life, sustenance, and spiritual fulfillment. Yet we, in our stubborn pride and limited understanding, too easily turn a blind eye and a deaf ear to this gracious offering. Some actively shield their hearts and minds from the transformative truth that this ultimate banquet holds, preferring instead to rely on our own flawed reasoning and worldly pursuits. We fail to comprehend the workings of the divine because we insist on clinging to our own narrow perspectives, willfully ignoring the boundless insight and illumination that God freely extends to us. This meal is not merely a ritual or tradition, but a wellspring of profound nourishment for the soul - a chance to partake in the very life and wisdom of the Almighty. Yet we carelessly reject this priceless gift, driven by our own selfish desires and limited faculties. If only we would open ourselves to receive this sacred provision with humility and trust, we would discover the unfathomable depth of God's love and the true path to fulfillment as human beings. But so often, we stubbornly cling to our own understanding, closing ourselves off from the eternal feast that our heavenly Father has so lovingly prepared for us.

The biblical story of Adam and Eve's expulsion from the Garden of Eden is a profound allegory about the human condition and our relationship with the divine. According to the Genesis account, God had placed the first man and woman in the lush, paradisiacal garden, where they enjoyed unfettered access to the "tree of life" - a symbolic representation of eternal, abundant life in communion with their Creator. However, the serpent's temptation leads Adam and Eve to "define goodness and life on their own terms" by disobeying God's command and partaking of the forbidden "tree of the knowledge of good and evil." In doing so, they arrogantly assert their autonomy and reject God's rightful authority, forfeiting the privileged status they had enjoyed. The consequence is their banishment from the garden, severing their direct connection to the source of life and forcing them to toil and struggle in a fallen, hostile world. This dramatic narrative encapsulates humanity's universal predicament - our innate desire for self-determination that leads us to stray from the path of divine wisdom and goodness, only to face the painful repercussions of our willful choices. The story reminds us that true flourishing is found not in autonomy, but in humble submission to the benevolent rule of our Maker, who alone can grant us access to the fullness of life.

The book I've written explores a deeply poignant and emotional story of a missing child, a tragedy that shakes the very foundations of the human experience. By crafting this narrative, I have tapped into a universal wellspring of fear, anguish, and the desperate longing for resolution that all parents and loved ones harbor in the face of such unimaginable loss. But my story does not merely dwell in the depths of this heartbreak - it also serves as a guiding light, leading the characters, and by extension the reader, on a profound spiritual journey back towards the grace and goodness of the divine.

The metaphorical "tree of life" becomes a symbolic representation of this path, a tangible manifestation of the eternal, restorative power of faith and righteous living. As the protagonists navigate the challenges and obstacles that stand between them and this sacred destination, we as the audience are invited to reflect on our own relationship with the Almighty, to consider how we might stray from the virtuous track and what it would take to return to the enlightened fold. Through this stirring narrative, you compel us to confront our own spiritual shortcomings, to seek atonement and to strive for a deeper, more meaningful connection with the divine - for it is only through this process of introspection and recommitment that we can truly find our way back to the goodness that God intends for all of His children.

In this powerful work, the call from God is unmistakably clear - the abhorrent practices of human trafficking and the disappearance of innocent children must come to an end. The author conveys a stark warning that if humanity continues to turn a blind eye to these egregious crimes, God himself will intervene with a plan far more severe and devastating than anything we can imagine. The message is unequivocal - those who are responsible for perpetuating these vile acts will face the full wrath of the divine. God can and will strip away all that which humans cling to, making it painfully evident that no earthly possession or pursuit is worth betraying the Almighty. Whether it be wealth, status, or material comforts, none of it will provide refuge or salvation from the righteous judgment of God. The stark reality is that once in the grip of the divine, there is no escape - you will never be able to remove yourself from the hands of the Almighty. The choice is clear - one must decide what is truly and eternally important, and take action to end the scourges of human trafficking and child exploitation. For God is a consuming fire when it comes to such grievous sins against the innocent, and His wrath will be unleashed if humanity fails to heed this urgent call to moral and ethical action.

* * *

Five

Chapter 5

The high-profile court case involving the mysterious death of Joslin Smith was a complex and drawn-out legal saga that played out in the coastal town of Saldahna, Vredenburg, located on the western shores of the country. The case had been delayed on two separate occasions, as the court struggled to gather sufficient evidence to prosecute the suspects, which included Joslin's own mother as well as three other individuals. Prosecutors were determined to build an airtight case, but the lack of conclusive proof made it challenging to move forward with the trial. Witnesses were scarce, forensic evidence was inconclusive, and the motives remained murky, leaving the judge and jury with little to go on as they attempted to unravel the tangled web of circumstances surrounding Joslin's untimely demise. The community watched with bated breath as the legal proceedings dragged on, the truth seemingly just out of reach. Tensions ran high, as the family and friends of the victim pleaded for justice, while the accused maintained their innocence in the face of the mounting public scrutiny. Ultimately, the court's inability to establish guilt beyond a reasonable doubt resulted in repeated delays, prolonging the agony for all involved and leaving the question of who was responsible for Joslin's death frustratingly unresolved, at least for the time being.

The police were tasked with maintaining order and keeping the community at a distance from the unfolding situation, but their methods often escalated tensions rather than quelling them. The interactions between law enforcement and the concerned citizens became increasingly confrontational, with the officers sometimes using heavy-handed tactics that went beyond what the circumstances warranted. Yet the community's demands were simple and clear - they merely sought answers and accountability regarding the fate of one of their own, a person named Joslin. The crowds gathered, their voices rising in a sorrowful chorus as they chanted Joslin's name over and over, pleading for information and demanding justice. It was a heartbreaking scene, as the people's anguish and frustration boiled over, directed at a system that seemed unwilling or unable to provide the answers they so desperately craved. The community's grief and outrage were palpable, their cries for Joslin and for justice echoing through the streets, a poignant reminder of the human cost when transparency and accountability are lacking. All the people wanted were answers about what had happened to Joslin - but as the standoff with the police dragged on, it became increasingly clear that those answers would not be forthcoming, at least not without a fight.

The crowd's cries for justice reverberated through the streets, a desperate plea for accountability in the case of Joslin. "We need justice for Joslin!" they would shout, their voices rising in a chorus of outrage and frustration. At other times, the chants would shift to a more personal, emotional refrain: "Joslin, our child!" This heart-wrenching plea underscored the deep connection the community felt to the individual at the center of this struggle. Tensions began to simmer under the surface of the crowd, a tangible sense of boiling anger and impatience. For too long, the people of Saldanha had felt that their concerns were falling on deaf ears, that the authorities were indifferent to their plight. Now, with the Joslin case unresolved, the simmering discontent had reached a fever pitch. The crowd knew that something had to give - the time for empty promises and inaction had long passed. They were determined to make their voices heard, to demand the justice they felt had been denied for far too long. The energy in the air was palpable, a tinderbox waiting to be ignited as the people of Saldanha refused to back down until their cries for accountability were finally The scene was one of chaos and confusion, as the crowd outside the courthouse repeatedly chanted, "We want Kelly's, we want Kelly's!" Their demands were directed at the mother, who remained tight-lipped, refusing to speak up and shed light on the mysterious case of Joslin. It was clear the police were at a loss, unsure of how to proceed with an investigation shrouded in the shadows of alleged witchcraft occurring in the town of Saldahna. The court, too, seemed blinded by the occult rumors swirling around the case, unable or unwilling to see past the veil of superstition to uncover the true facts. The uproar from the impatient mob only added to the sense of unease, as they grew increasingly frustrated by the lack of answers and transparency.

It was a powder keg situation, with tensions running high and the authorities seemingly paralyzed, uncertain of how to navigate the murky waters of a case that appeared to defy logic and reason. The mother, holding the key to unraveling the mystery, remained silent, perhaps out of fear, or perhaps out of a desire to protect some deeper, darker secret. Whatever the reason, her refusal to speak only fueled the public's demand for answers, creating an impasse that threatened to boil over into something even more chaotic and unpredictable.

The people were growing increasingly frustrated and incensed as the court proceedings dragged on for months with no resolution in sight. What should have been a straightforward case had become mired in bureaucratic delays and drawn-out investigations, much to the ire of the public. Five long months had passed since the initial incident, and still the wheels of justice seemed to be turning at a glacial pace, leaving the aggrieved citizens feeling powerless and betrayed by a system that was supposed to work swiftly and efficiently to deliver fair outcomes. The investigators, with their meticulous but time-consuming methods, were perceived by the enraged populace as obstructing the path to justice, prolonging the anguish and denying closure to those impacted by the events in question. Tempers flared as the people watched helplessly, their righteous anger building with each passing day, as the case became mired in red tape and legal maneuverings rather than finding a timely and satisfactory conclusion. The public's trust in the judicial process was hanging by a thread, their patience exhausted by the interminable delays that seemed to prioritize bureaucratic procedure over the actual delivery of justice that the community so desperately craved.

The comunity were left frustrated and perplexed as the forensics team informed the court that their investigation had not yet yielded the conclusive evidence needed to make a solid case. Despite the high hopes they had initially held, the police now found themselves at a standstill, with no clear path forward. The lack of definitive forensic findings only compounded the mystery, leaving gaping holes in their understanding of what had truly transpired. With no new leads or breakthroughs to grasp onto, the investigators were forced to confront the unsettling reality that the perpetrator may have covered their tracks all too well. It was as if a veil of darkness had descended, obscuring the truth and rendering the officers helpless to see what was right in front of them. The case seemed to have hit a dead end, the elusive answers they sought stubbornly evading their every effort. Faced with this roadblock, the police could only hope that some unforeseen development or overlooked clue would soon emerge to shed light on the shadows shrouding this perplexing mystery. Until then, they would have to grapple with the frustration of an investigation that, for the moment, appeared to have stalled before the job was fully done. Over a year had elapsed since Joslin's mysterious disappearance, and still no trace of the missing person had been uncovered, leaving investigators and the community baffled and desperate for answers. The case had become a frustrating quagmire, with no clear leads or obvious suspects to pursue. Detectives had meticulously combed through every available piece of evidence, interviewed countless witnesses, and followed up on even the most tenuous of tips, but the trail had gone cold, leaving them grasping at straws in their attempts to unravel the perplexing circumstances surrounding Joslin's vanishing.

Compounding the difficulty was the distinct lack of any concrete information about Joslin's whereabouts or final movements prior to their disappearance. Without a shred of physical evidence or credible eyewitness accounts, the investigators found themselves stymied, unable to discern even the most basic details that could provide crucial clues. The case had become a maddening puzzle with too many missing pieces, leaving the frustrated law enforcement team at an impasse despite their tireless efforts.

As the calendar continued to tick by with no resolution, the community grew increasingly anxious and despondent, the mystery surrounding Joslin's fate weighing heavily on the hearts and minds of all those invested in seeing justice served. The prolonged silence from any leads or breakthroughs had spawned a palpable sense of dread, with whispers of foul play and ominous speculation running rampant. The longer Joslin remained missing, the more the hope for a positive outcome seemed to fade, as the case became mired in an infuriating and seemingly insurmountable quagmire that defied all attempts at unraveling its disturbing secrets.

In the outskirts of the bustling city of Saldahna, there lived a dedicated councilor whose heart was fully aligned with the people. This steadfast individual, deeply committed to the wellbeing of the Saldahnan community, would faithfully attend the third court case that was set to take place. Recognizing the importance of transparency and keeping the citizens informed, this councilor made it a priority to gather and disseminate crucial details about the upcoming proceedings. On July 15th, 2024, the third hearing in this significant legal matter was scheduled, and this councilor ensured that the people of Saldahna were well-prepared and knowledgeable about what to expect. Through tireless efforts and a genuine concern for the community, this councilor became a trusted conduit of information, bridging the gap between the formalities of the judicial system and the everyday lives of the Saldahnan populace.

When the court case had finally concluded, there was still no tangible progress made in resolving the matter at hand. The defendant, visibly frustrated, addressed the gathered community and relayed the disappointing news. The court, it seemed, had decided that the case required further deliberation and had scheduled another hearing on a future date. This was an unsatisfactory outcome for all involved, who had been eagerly anticipating a decisive ruling. The defendant expressed their intent to escalate the case to a higher judicial authority, in the hopes that a court of greater jurisdiction could provide a more conclusive and authoritative resolution. The community members listened intently, their expressions a mix of dismay and determination, as they processed this latest development in the long-running legal battle. It was clear that the path to justice remained arduous and uncertain, with the promise of more court appearances and legal maneuvering on the horizon. Nevertheless, the defendant vowed to persevere, buoyed by the unwavering support of the local community, who were prepared to see this fight through to the end, no matter how many more court dates and appeals lay ahead. Despite the intense investigation into the disappearance of Joslin Smith, there remained a maddening lack of concrete evidence to shed light on what had become of the young woman. The authorities were left utterly perplexed, grasping at straws as they combed through every possible lead and scoured the area where she was last seen, yet finding themselves no closer to uncovering the truth. It was a frustrating and demoralizing situation for the dedicated detectives working the case, who had pursued every conceivable avenue only to hit dead end after dead end. With no eyewitnesses, no ransom demands, and no signs of foul play, the mysterious vanishing of Joslin Smith had become a vexing conundrum that seemed to defy all logical explanation. The longer the case went unsolved, the more it ate away at the investigators, who knew that with each passing day, the trail was growing colder and the likelihood of finding Joslin alive grew more and more remote. It was a disaster of the highest order - a complete and utter failure of the system to protect a vulnerable citizen and provide answers to her devastated family. The lack of evidence was maddening, leaving the authorities feeling helpless and the community on edge, desperate for closure that stubbornly remained out of reach.

The councilor recounted a troubling scene he had witnessed in the courtroom, where the mother of Joslin and her associates stood as suspected perpetrators. Despite the gravity of the situation, the councilor noted that these individuals appeared almost untouchable, exuding an unsettling air of confidence and even satisfaction. As they stood before the court, the mother and her friends seemed to wear an unsettling smile, their demeanor suggesting a level of comfort and even glee at finding themselves in this position. The councilor was struck by the apparent lack of remorse or fear, as if they believed themselves to be above the law and immune to the consequences of their alleged actions. This brazen attitude in the face of serious allegations only served to further unsettle the councilor, who could not help but wonder at the complex web of privilege, power, and corruption that may have shielded these individuals from true accountability. The councilor's observations painted a disturbing picture of a justice system that at times appears to favor the wealthy and well-connected, allowing them to evade the very rules and punishments that apply to the common citizen. This troubling dynamic, if left unchecked, threatened to further erode public trust in the fairness and impartiality of the legal proceedings.

This world we inhabit can often feel like a cold, disconnected place where compassion and empathy have taken a backseat to indifference and self-absorption. It's a reality that strikes at the core of our humanity and leaves many of us grappling with a profound sense of loneliness and despair. How did we stray so far from treating one another with the dignity, kindness, and concern that our shared condition as fellow human beings demands? The loss of that essential thread of common understanding is truly heartbreaking, bringing forth tears of anguish from the depths of our souls.

We live in an age where it can feel like no one truly cares about the lived experiences and innermost feelings of those around them. People seem so caught up in their own lives, their own struggles, their own desires, that they've forgotten how to look beyond themselves and extend a hand, an ear, a shoulder to those who are hurting. This epidemic of apathy is a tragic deviation from our innate capacity for empathy - the ability to emotionally connect with and seek to alleviate the suffering of others.

Where did we go so wrong as a society that we've become so insular, so detached, so unwilling to feel the pain of our fellow man as our own? It's a question that haunts the conscience, for without that fundamental human bond, we risk losing touch with our very essence as a species. The tears that well up from within speak to a longing to recapture that lost sense of community, that lost understanding that we are all in this together, that each of our lives has value and deserves to be treated with compassion. If only we could reawaken that dormant capacity for care and connection, perhaps we could begin to heal the fractures that have torn us apart.

It's truly a heartbreaking and tragic situation when someone's life is cut short or irreparably harmed by the cruel, callous actions of another person. The sheer weight of the sadness and injustice is almost overwhelming to contemplate. How can it be that those who commit such heinous, unfeeling crimes are sometimes able to evade the full consequences of their misdeeds? It speaks to a deeply flawed and unjust system that allows the perpetrators of unspeakable acts to in some cases walk away with relatively light sentences, while the victims and their loved ones are left to grapple with the devastating aftermath for the rest of their lives. This sense of an imbalance, where the wicked seem to prosper while the innocent suffer, can make one question the very foundations of the society we live in.

As a close-knit community, we clung to the hope that our beloved Joslin Smith was still alive, despite the lack of a body or definitive evidence of her fate. With unwavering faith, we gathered at the local church day after day, drawing strength from one another's prayers and determination. The image of Joslin's striking green eyes was seared into our collective memory, fueling our relentless search for any sign of the vibrant young woman who had disappeared without a trace. We refused to give up, buoyed by the belief that as long as her body remained undiscovered, there was still a chance she could be found alive and returned to us, safe and sound. This shared conviction, this driving force of hope, galvanized us as a community to scour every inch of the surrounding area, to follow up on even the most tenuous of leads, to never cease in our efforts to bring our "green-eyed angel" home. In the face of the unknown, we clung to our faith, our compassion, and our unwavering commitment to one another, steadfast in our conviction that Joslin was out there, waiting to be found and welcomed back into the embrace of her loving community.

With the fervent expectation pulsing within our hearts, we clung to the belief that she might somehow, against all odds, reappear before us. Despite the bleak circumstances and the seemingly insurmountable obstacles, we refused to give in to despair. Instead, we held fast to the conviction that God's power and divine providence extended far beyond the limits of our own narrow perspectives and finite understanding. In the face of a situation that appeared utterly hopeless to the human mind, we steadfastly maintained our faith that the Almighty was still capable of accomplishing the impossible. Though the challenges seemed to loom ever larger, obscuring any glimmer of hope, we remained steadfast in our resolve, our spirits buoyed by the unwavering certainty that the Heavenly Father could and would intervene in ways that transcended our mortal comprehension. Even as the days stretched on with no sign of her return, we continued to lift our hearts in prayer, pleading for a miracle that would defy all earthly logic and reasoning. For we knew, with every fiber of our being, that the same God who had parted the mighty seas and raised the dead held the power to make the impossible possible, if only we clung to our belief with unwavering faith.

As the child's innocent eyes gazed up at me, a flurry of thoughts raced through my mind. How could anyone dare to harm such a pure, vulnerable being? A child deserves to be showered with love, affection, and the warmth of a caring embrace - not subjected to cruelty, pain, and the darker impulses that can sometimes lurk within the human heart. It's a tragic reality that life is not always the idyllic, carefree experience it should be for a child. Too often, the world can be a harsh, unforgiving place, shaped by the bitter, selfish choices of adults whose capacity for compassion has been eroded. A child's tender, unwavering trust is so easily shattered when they encounter the ugliness that some people are capable of. It's heartbreaking to witness the light in their eyes begin to dim, replaced by a guarded wariness that no child should ever have to develop. We have an obligation to shield the young from life's cruelties, to nurture them with unconditional love and support them as they navigate the challenges of growing up. Yet there are those who callously disregard this sacred duty, inflicting untold damage that can scar a child's soul forever. It's a sobering truth that the very people entrusted to care for a child can also be the source of their deepest wounds.

The disappearance of Joslin Smith was a tragic event that brought a pressing issue to the forefront of our minds as parents - the need to be ever-vigilant in protecting our children. Prior to this incident, many of us had perhaps taken our children's safety for granted, assuming that as long as we loved them and provided for their basic needs, they would remain safe and secure. However, Joslin's mysterious vanishing served as a sobering wake-up call, reminding us that danger can lurk in the most unexpected places. In that moment, the rose-colored glasses came off, and we were forced to confront the harsh reality that our little ones are vulnerable, and that we must be proactive in safeguarding them at all times. Gone were the days of casually letting them play outside unattended or allowing them to wander off on their own. Now, we found ourselves hyper-vigilant, our eyes constantly scanning the environment for any potential threats. We became fiercely protective, unwilling to let our children out of our sight for even a second, lest they too fall victim to some unseen peril. This heightened state of alertness, born from the anguish of Joslin's disappearance, has become the new normal for us as parents. We are determined to learn from this tragedy and ensure that our own children never suffer a similar fate, no matter the cost to our own peace of mind.

Joslin's Smith's name has become far more than just a simple moniker - it is a symbol, a rallying cry, and a testament to the power of one life to enact profound change. Though her tragic disappearance was a devastating event that shook her community, Joslin's legacy has lived on in profound and impactful ways. She has become a hero to countless parents who now vigilantly watch over their children, ever-mindful of the dangers that lurk in the shadows. Joslin's story has brought a crucial message to light - that trusting others with your child, no matter how well-intentioned they may seem, can have devastating consequences. But perhaps her most lasting impact has been in highlighting the grave risks posed by parents struggling with addiction. Joslin's fate made it devastatingly clear that the all-consuming grip of substance abuse can drive even a loving parent to unthinkable actions. Her disappearance was a heartbreaking reminder that a person under the influence of drugs is no longer in full control of their faculties or their actions, capable of harming their own child in ways a sober, rational person never would. Though Joslin's life was cut short, her memory lives on, inspiring parents to be more cautious, to be more vigilant, and to never underestimate the dangers that can arise when a child is entrusted to someone whose judgment is impaired. Joslin Smith may be gone, but her name and her message will echo through the ages, ensuring that her sacrifice was not in vain.

Joslin Smith's remarkable journey to becoming a national hero was marked by her unwavering faith and divine purpose. As a deeply religious woman, Joslin believed she had been anointed by God with a special power to unite her community and ultimately, her entire nation. Through her tireless efforts, she successfully brought together churches and congregations of all denominations, fostering a newfound spirit of unity and cooperation. But Joslin's true legacy lay in her ability to reintroduce God into the political sphere, which had long pushed faith to the sidelines. In a time of great turmoil and division, Joslin recognized the crucial role that spirituality and moral principles must play in guiding a nation. She became a vocal advocate, using her powerful oratory skills to remind political leaders of their responsibility to uphold the teachings of the divine. Joslin's message resonated profoundly with the people, who had grown weary of the disconnect between government and the sacred. As she breathed new life into the relationship between church and state, Joslin emerged as a beacon of hope for a nation teetering on the brink of collapse. Her remarkable feats of leadership and faith cemented her status as a true hero, not just for her local community, but for an entire country that had rediscovered the transformative power of God's grace.

The disappearance of this young girl sent shockwaves through the nation, serving as a powerful reminder of the urgent need to address the crisis of missing children in our society. Her case highlighted the heartbreaking reality that far too many families have had to endure - the agonizing uncertainty and pain of a loved one vanishing without a trace. Through this tragedy, she has become a poignant symbol, her very absence speaking volumes about the failings of our justice system to protect the most vulnerable. Her disappearance lays bare the systemic flaws that allow cases like hers to fall through the cracks, the lack of resources and coordination that hampers effective investigations, and the distressing reality that justice all too often remains elusive for the families left behind. This girl's story has become a clarion call, demanding that we as a nation recommit ourselves to safeguarding our children and ensuring that when they vanish, the full weight of the law and the unwavering resolve of our communities are brought to bear. Her legacy, etched in the void she has left, is a challenge to fix the deep-seated problems that allowed this to happen - to rebuild a justice system that is truly just, one that operates with the utmost urgency and compassion when a child disappears. Only then can we honor her memory by preventing others from suffering the same heartbreak, and restore a fundamental promise of safety and security that every child deserves.

She made it clear that God wants to be part of us, not separate from us. We are His creation, made in His image, and He desires an intimate, personal relationship with each of His children. The tragic disappearance of young Joslin Smith was a heartbreaking reminder that too many vulnerable children have been lost, stolen, and sold - a fate that no child should ever have to endure. It's a shocking reality that cries out for justice and change. She passionately proclaimed that God has had enough of this injustice, this exploitation of the innocent. Enough is enough, He declares. We are His beloved, created in love to live in love - not to be reduced to mere commodities, to be callously bought and sold. We are humans, blessed with hearts that can feel, minds that can reason, and souls that long for connection with the divine. We must remember our sacred worth and live accordingly, treating ourselves and others with the dignity, compassion, and respect that our shared humanity demands. For we are not stones, but flesh and blood, imbued with the capacity to show kindness, to offer mercy, to pursue righteousness. This is the call that God places upon our lives - to reflect His character, to be His hands and feet in a world that so desperately needs His redeeming touch. Let us heed this clarion call and rise to the occasion, honoring God and one another as the precious, priceless beings we are.

It is our solemn duty as human beings to protect one another from the malevolent forces that seek to corrupt and destroy the sanctity of our existence. For out there in the shadows lurk unspeakable evils, twisted entities with eyes that glow a demonic red, like the smoldering embers of a hellfire. These wicked terrors are driven by a singular, insatiable desire to extinguish the radiant beauty that graces our world. They would rend asunder the very fabric of our society, snuffing out the light of hope and plunging us into a realm of unrelenting darkness, were it not for the steadfast resolve of those willing to stand as bulwarks against such malignant influences. Each of us bears the responsibility to be vigilant, to be the watchful guardians who shield the innocent and vulnerable from the predations of these monster-like figures. Through our unity, our compassion, and our refusal to surrender in the face of such pernicious threats, we can ensure that the wonder and splendor that imbues our shared existence is preserved, flourishing for generations to come. It is a sacred trust, a noble calling that demands our utmost commitment, for the alternative - to allow these wicked terrors to run rampant - is a fate too grim to even contemplate.

We must take the fullest measure of responsibility in the face of this profound evil that has taken hold, and through our steadfast acts of faith, we must work tirelessly to strip these malicious forces of their power and influence. This is not a task to be taken lightly, for the darkness that we confront is deep-rooted and pervasive, woven into the very fabric of our society. Yet, it is our sacred duty to shine the light of righteousness and truth into these shadowy corners, to expose the corruption and deceit that have allowed this scourge to fester. With unwavering conviction and moral fortitude, we must marshal every resource at our disposal – our voices, our actions, our unyielding spirits – to wage an uncompromising campaign against this pernicious threat. In doing so, we assert our fundamental right to live in a world governed by justice, compassion, and the triumph of the human spirit over the forces of wickedness. This is no easy undertaking, but it is one that we must embrace with unwavering determination, for the stakes are nothing less than the very soul of our shared existence.

Chapter 5

Through our acts of faith, steadfast and true, we will reclaim what has been taken from us, and emerge victorious in this eternal struggle between light and dark.

99

* * *

Chapter 6

The mysterious disappearance of Joslin Smith has left the tight-knit community of Saldahna reeling, with no clear answers or leads to provide any sense of closure. Joslin, a beloved local resident known for her warm smile and tireless community involvement, vanished without a trace several weeks ago, sparking a frantic search that has so far yielded no clues as to her whereabouts. The unsettling silence surrounding her disappearance has only amplified the anguish and uncertainty felt by her devastated friends, family, and neighbors, who are desperate to uncover what happened and bring Joslin home safely. Day by day, the community's collective grief deepens as the investigation hits one dead end after another, with no solid evidence or witnesses to shed light on Joslin's inexplicable vanishing. The lack of progress has only fueled rampant speculation and fearful imagination within the town, leaving residents increasingly distraught and plagued by a maddening inability to find answers or find closure in their mourning. As the community continues its grueling wait for any new developments, the gaping hole left by Joslin's disappearance looms larger, underscoring the heartbreaking reality that, for now, the mystery of her vanishing shows no signs of being resolved.

The young child's story is indeed a heartbreaking one, a tragic tale that shines a light on the harsh, unforgiving realities that far too many innocent youths are forced to endure in this world. Though she was just a small, naive child, barely old enough to understand the complexities of the world around her, her fate took a devastating turn that she could never have anticipated or prepared for. As a vulnerable, impressionable child who so desperately needed the loving guidance, unwavering support, and steadfast protection that every young person deserves, she instead found herself targeted and exploited by the dark, predatory forces that lurk within the shadows of society. Identity thieves, cunning criminals, and other morally bankrupt individuals who seek to prey upon the most innocent and defenseless members of our communities - these were the forces that converged upon this poor child, robbing her of her childhood, her sense of safety and security, and her very right to live a normal, carefree life like her peers. With her tender years and trusting nature, she stood no chance against such vicious, unscrupulous adversaries, and the traumatic fallout of their abhorrent actions will undoubtedly haunt and scar her for the rest of her days. It is a heartbreaking reality that no child should ever have to face, and yet the sad truth is that this tragic scenario plays out time and time again, as vulnerable young lives are callously destroyed by those who would exploit them for their own selfish gain. This child's story is a sobering reminder of the work that remains to be done in order to protect our youth and ensure that every child has the opportunity to grow and thrive in a safe, nurturing environment, free from the threat of such devastating harm.

The thunderous call from the divine echoes through the heavens, a clarion cry demanding an end to the heinous scourge of human trafficking that has plagued humanity for far too long. This abhorrent practice, where the most vulnerable among us are cruelly ripped from their homes and families, reduced to mere commodities to be bought, sold, and exploited, stands in direct defiance of the sacred sanctity of human life. The Almighty's righteous anger burns with an intensity that cannot be ignored, for every life stolen, every soul crushed under the weight of this monstrous industry, is an affront to the very fabric of creation. This is no mere crime, but a violation of the natural order, a tearing asunder of the bonds that should unite us all as children of the same Creator. The divine decree is clear: the murder of innocents, the theft of lives that are not ours to take - these grave transgressions must come to an end, for they strike at the heart of our shared humanity. The time has come to heed this urgent summons, to rise up and extinguish the darkness that has cast its pall over our world, and to restore the light of justice, compassion, and the sacred dignity of every human being. Only then can we begin to heal the wounds inflicted by this scourge and fulfill the Almighty's vision of a world where all people are free to live, love, and flourish as intended.

The issue of human trafficking and the disappearance of

individuals is a grave concern that demands urgent attention from governing authorities. The tragic story of Joslin Smith's disappearance on the west coast of South Africa serves as a harrowing example of why governments must take stronger, more decisive action to combat these heinous crimes and uphold the rule of law. Joslin's fate, allowed to unfold by the apparent lack of proper safeguards and enforcement, has now become a wake-up call for the nation - a stark reminder that complacency in the face of such dangers is unacceptable. Porous borders, inadequate investigative resources, and lenient penalties for perpetrators have all too often enabled human traffickers and other malicious actors to operate with impunity, shattering the lives of vulnerable individuals and leaving grieving families desperate for answers and justice. If this tragedy is to serve any purpose, it must be to galvanize lawmakers and law enforcement to take concrete, comprehensive steps to strengthen protections, elevate penalties, and coordinate cross-border efforts to dismantle these criminal networks. Only then can the abhorrent practice of human trafficking be stamped out, and the heartbreaking occurrences of unexplained disappearances become a thing of the past. Joslin's story, though wrought with sorrow, must now inspire a renewed commitment to the fundamental principles of human rights and public safety that any just society is built upon.

* * *

Seven

Chapter 7

The mysterious disappearance of Joslin Smith has undoubtedly left an indelible mark on the collective consciousness of the community. While the tragedy of her vanishing will forever haunt those who knew and loved her, it has also served as a catalyst for profound change and introspection. Through the darkness of this unimaginable event, Joslin's story has paradoxically opened up new avenues of understanding and connection. In the wake of her disappearance, disparate factions - from local authorities to religious institutions to concerned individuals - have come together in a unified effort to uncover the truth and seek justice. This collaborative spirit has spawned innovative approaches, with previously unheralded talents emerging to contribute in meaningful ways, whether through song, written word, or artistic expression. What was once an unspeakable loss has now become a wellspring of hope, as the community rallies to honor

Joslin's memory and find solace in the unexpected gifts that have blossomed from the most painful of circumstances. Though the ache of her absence will never fully heal, Joslin's legacy has transcended the confines of her disappearance, becoming a poignant testament to the resilience of the human spirit and the transformative power of adversity.

The disappearance of Joslin Smith captivated the nation and shed a harsh light on the dark realities that can lurk beneath the surface of society. The story revealed the heartless and cruel aspects of human existence, where the vulnerable can be callously discarded and forgotten. It exposed the grim truth that, in this world, there are those who would selfishly disregard the wellbeing of others, driven by their own twisted motives and lack of empathy. However, amidst this bleak landscape, the Joslin Smith saga also showcased the remarkable capacity of the human spirit to rise up in unity and love. As the community rallied together, bound by their shared faith and compassion, it became clear that even in the face of unimaginable tragedy, people have an innate desire to support one another, to seek justice, and to uphold the sacred values that make us human. The outpouring of solidarity demonstrated that, at our core, we yearn to serve a higher purpose, to come together under the guidance of a higher power, and to affirm that the darkest expressions of our nature can be overcome by the bright flame of our shared humanity. Joslin's story, in all its heartbreak and hope, revealed the full spectrum of what it means to be human - the capacity for both cruelty and kindness, selfishness and selflessness, despair and resilience. It was a stark reminder that even in our most trying moments, the indomitable spirit of community and the transcendent power of love can shine through, guiding us towards a more just, compassionate, and meaningful existence.

The world watched with bated breath as the story of Joslin Smith's mysterious disappearance unraveled, captivated by the deeper truths that lay beneath the surface. In the midst of the uncertainty and speculation, it became increasingly clear that a divine hand was at work, guiding the events in a way that would ultimately serve a greater purpose. The selection of the country's leaders during this tumultuous time was no mere coincidence, but rather a testament to God's sovereign plan. These were individuals whose moral compasses had been honed and strengthened, their characters forged in the crucible of adversity. They were the chosen ones, imbued with a clarity of vision and an unwavering commitment to lead the nation down the path that the Almighty had ordained. Their actions, though at times met with skepticism or resistance, were infused with a higher purpose, a divine mandate to steer the country towards the destiny that had been set for it. As the details of Joslin Smith's disappearance.

The disappearance of Joslin Smith created a sense of urgency and crisis that brought forth true leaders from within the community. These were individuals who rose to the occasion, driven by a genuine concern for the well-being of their fellow citizens. Amongst them was Gayton MacKenzie, a politician whose heart was firmly rooted in the needs of the people. Unlike many of his counterparts who were primarily concerned with personal gain or political agendas, MacKenzie was a leader who truly empathized with the struggles and fears of the community. He sprang into action, marshaling resources, coordinating search efforts, and providing a calming presence amidst the chaos. His unwavering commitment to finding Joslin and supporting the affected families stood in stark contrast to the self-serving nature of many politicians. MacKenzie's leadership was defined by his ability to put people first, to listen intently, and to make decisions that prioritized the greater good over narrow interests. In a time of uncertainty and anguish, his emergence as a true leader, driven by compassion rather than political expediency, provided a beacon of hope and reassurance for a community in desperate need. The Joslin Smith disappearance had the power to bring out the worst in people, but it also revealed the best – individuals like Gayton MacKenzie, who embodied the qualities of authentic, servant-hearted leadership that the situation so urgently demanded.

The disappearance of Joslin Smith seemed to bring forth a wave of true spiritual leaders who arose to provide comfort, guidance, and a message of hope during this difficult time. Figures like Pastor Leo dos Santos, Pastor Fransico "coffee", and Prophet Leon emerged as powerful voices, offering prayers, counseling, and even prophetic insights that resonated deeply with the community. Prophet Leon's prophesy over Joslin's mother Kelly, which came to pass in just three days as he foretold, demonstrated a profound spiritual gift and connection that captivated the people. Beyond these charismatic preachers, other notable leaders like Prophet Tania B, Dj. Stacy Prophet J.J together with their team and the Men of War , wellknown for their deliverance mission under the youth, also stepped up, driven by a genuine passion for love and a concern for Joslin's wellbeing. These were not self-serving individuals, but rather selfless servants who placed the community's needs above their own. Leaving their own families and comfort behind to rather search for a missing child, this is humanity in the fullness of Love, Even artists like Temple boys, Ziggy, Mp, Fransiena, and many others took hands and join , worship singers appeared on stage, using their platforms to raise a praise and worship as awareness and show that they too cared deeply about Joslin's disappearance. Even new songs was born during through this time and perhaps the most inspiring figure to emerge was

Oom Biza vannie Kaap, a leader who led by powerful example, embodying the very values he espoused. Through all of this, one can learn that God truly does care for each and every one of us, and desires for us to be united in love, honesty, and faith. It is a reminder that His grace, mercy, and hope are everlasting, and that we must let go of our own limited understanding to make space for Him to work. While material wealth may provide for our physical needs, the true riches lie in the love, compassion, and spiritual nourishment that these leaders freely gave during Joslin's time of crisis.

The disappearance of Joslin Smith has understandably caused great concern and anguish among all those who knew and admired her. Joslin was no ordinary individual - she was a shining beacon of hope and inspiration, chosen to become a true hero not just for our nation, but for the entire world and even the vast expanse of the universe beyond. Her name carries profound meaning and significance, representing the very best of humanity's potential. We must remain steadfast in our faith that Joslin is still alive somewhere, despite the troubling circumstances of her disappearance. Each and every one of us has an obligation to continue praying, searching, and seeking any information that could lead to her safe return. Joslin's story has captivated people globally, for she was destined for greatness - to make an indelible mark on the world through her courage, compassion, and unparalleled spirit. She is a beacon of hope that illuminates the darkness, inspiring us to never give up in the face of adversity. As long as there is breath in our lungs and fire in our hearts, we will honor Joslin Smith and everything she represents, for she is a true hero whose legacy will reverberate throughout the ages, echoing across the cosmos.

As you has notice in this powerful and thought-provoking book, the I provided a deeply Godly insightful exploration of the tragic disappearance of Joslin Smith, delving into the matter through the profound lens of divine providence. Through their vivid and emotionally resonant writing, I invited readers to bear witness to this harrowing case, guiding us to consider it not merely as an isolated incident, but as a sobering reflection of the darker forces at work in our world.

By sharing this intimate perspective, I skillfully weaves a narrative that transcends the specifics of Joslin's story, speaking to the wider epidemic of human trafficking, lost children, and unsolved cases that continue to haunt our societies.

Infused with a sense of spiritual urgency, my words challenge us to raise our collective voices, to look upon one another with renewed empathy and purpose, and to confront the shadowy powers that prey upon the vulnerable.

Ultimately, this book stands as a poignant call to action, inspiring readers to find hope in the face of darkness and to rededicate themselves to the noble cause of justice, compassion, and the preservation of human dignity.

May the profound insights contained within these pages embolden us all to walk the path of righteousness, guided by the grace of the divine.

Thank you for reading this book I hope that is was well inspired to every one as I shared very deep insight on the matter of Joslin Smith's disappearance through the eyes of God's presents.

Written by:
Shane Marquin van Rooyen.

* * *